AF870565

NAILING THE BAR

HOW TO WRITE ESSAYS FOR CONTRACTS & UCC LAW SCHOOL AND BAR EXAMS

What to Say and How to Say It.

Tim Tyler, Ph.D.
Attorney at Law

Published by: ***Practical Step Press***
A Division of
LEGAL BOOKS DISTRIBUTING

--www.PracticalStepPress.com--

ISBN 978-1-936160-01-3

What to Say and How to Say It

This book is a "How To" guide of practical information needed to succeed on LAW SCHOOL EXAMS and BAR EXAMS on **Contracts** and the **UCC**.[1] It is based entirely on **common law and broadly adopted modern views** applicable to exams in every State.

This is a "cook book" approach focused on the <u>mechanics</u> and <u>substance</u> needed to write passing law school essays; **WHAT TO SAY and HOW TO SAY IT.**

EVERYTHING you NEED to SUCCEED is provided without unnecessary baggage.

The central focus of this book is "NAILING" the elements. "NAILING" means to cite the **ELEMENTS OF PROOF** the moving party (movant) must prove at each stage of a legal action. At each stage the "matter at issue" is either a CAUSE OF ACTION or an AFFIRMATIVE DEFENSE that has been raised by the movant. To "nail the elements" you must know what the REQUIRED ELEMENTS OF PROOF are, say what they are, and explain HOW the movant can prove them with the given facts, or else explain WHY they cannot be proven.

Brilliance is not needed nor even enough to succeed in law school, to pass the Bar Exam, or to be a lawyer. Many attorneys are not brilliant, but they succeeded in law school. And there is nothing so common as brilliant people that have failed law school. **The REASON** is **THEY LEARNED EVERYTHING EXCEPT** the one important thing -- **HOW TO PASS THE EXAMS.**

This book gives you **EVERY important issue, EVERY important rule** and **EVERY important definition** you need along with practice questions and **sample answers.**

This book uses a methodical, practical, step-by-step approach to create issue analysis that works. It may seem mechanical, but it produces passing essay answers. This method is called "**NAILING THE ELEMENTS**" (Chapter 10). Whether you are completing the first year of law school or preparing for a Bar Exam this simple approach will help you succeed.

This book tells you **how to outline** your essay answer (Chapter 3), **how to spot issues** (Chapter 4), **how to avoid wasting time** (Chapter 5) and **budgeting time** on your essay (Chapter 7).

This book gives you **EVERY IMPORTANT DEFINITION** you need to know for law school exams on **CONTRACTS** and the **UCC** (Appendix A.) It shows you **EXAMPLES** of good and bad essay approaches, and it give you **PRACTICE QUESTIONS** complete with **SAMPLE ANSWERS** and **EXPLANATIONS**.

This book necessarily omits discussion of many intricate details of the law that are explained in Nailing the Bar's "Simple Contracts and UCC Outline". But **EVERYTHING YOU REALLY NEED TO KNOW to prepare for your Contracts and UCC exams is in this ONE book.**

---

[1] This book covers UCC Articles 1, 2, 3 and 9. Bar exams vary between States. For example, California only tests on UCC Articles 1 and 2 while New York also tests on Articles 3 and 9.

Table of Contents

Chapter 1: Why Essays are Critical

In law school the ability to write a proper essay answer is critical. On your first day of law school look at the people on your left, your right and three people in front of you. At the end of the first year of law school two of those six people will be GONE. By the end of law school two more of those six people will be GONE. And in many States only one of those six people can pass the Bar examination on the first try. **Follow the instructions in this book and it will be you!**

The difference between the ONE student who succeeds and the FIVE students that fail is the ability to write a proper law school essay answer. It is both necessary to succeed in law school and essential to passing the Bar Exams.

Being smart is not enough. Everyone in law school is smart. Some of the students in your first-year law school class may seem stupid. Do not be deceived. They could not have all gotten into law school if they were as dumb as they look.

In fact, some of the attractive, sophisticated and eloquent students will be the first to fail. Your grade in law school, and on the Bar exams, depends on only ONE FACTOR. It is not what you look like, or what you talk like. It is what you PUT ON PAPER.

LEARN TO WRITE A PROPER ESSAY and your entire law school experience will be enjoyable, your class standing will improve at every turn and you will pass the Bar upon completion of law school.

FAIL TO ADOPT GOOD ESSAY FORM and your life will be Hell! You will fail law school, you will never become an attorney, and you will owe thousands of dollars in student loans that you cannot escape in bankruptcy. The sooner you learn what to do the better off you will be.

The Grading Key IS the Key. Law school exams and Bar exams are graded by means of a grading "key". The Grading Key is the guide the professor (or Bar reader) uses so that grades are as consistent as possible.

The Grading Key is a list of the ISSUES you are expected to recognize and address and the RULES of law you are expected to cite.

Certain FACTS are mentioned in the essay question, and the grading key reflects those facts that you should comment on in your ANALYSIS.

Finally, for each issue, you must state a CONCLUSION.

IRAC. This essay structure -- Issue, Rule, Analysis and Conclusion -- is referred to as the IRAC approach to essay writing.

State the Required Issues. The Grading Key has certain REQUIRED ISSUES. If your essay answer lists and analyzes all of the required issues, your essay is usually given a score of 70 points. For each required issue that you skip, your grade is reduced.

It is critical for you to recognize and state the proper area of law raised by the facts.

Generally, the required issues are worth about 5 points each. Your essay grade will be reduced (from 70) by 5 points for each required issue that you fail to discuss. Some issues, such as murder and negligence are worth 10 or more points, depending on the question.

How Graders Look at your Essays. In law school essays are generally graded by the professor, and she or he will read your essay more closely to see if you have developed an understanding of the fine points of the black letter law. Since the law school professor looks more carefully at your answer, you may be able to deviate farther from the IRAC approach without suffering a penalty. This is unfortunate because the Bar Exam essays are graded with close adherence to the IRAC approach.

When the grader first picks up your essay answer, she often starts by flipping through it to get a feel for the quality of you answer based on its appearance. If your writing is messy, your issues are not clear and you are disorganized, the grader will not be given a good first impression. Mentally, she will stop thinking "possible 70" and start thinking "probable 60". She will not waste a lot of time on your essay if it is an obvious loser.

The grader will next look at the last page of your answer to see if you ran out of time. If so, the grader may give you a grade of 45 or 50 without even bothering to read your essay at all.

So NEVER "LOOK" like you ran out of time!! ALWAYS have a "conclusion" at the end of your essay to make it appear you finished with adequate time. NEVER say "out of time!" at the end of your essay. NEVER put a big, garbled, frantic, scribbled mess at the end of the essay. NEVER write out an outline of the issues that you didn't have time to discuss. If you do these things you might as well write, "I AM STUPID; PLEASE SHOOT ME."

Aspire to be Adequate on Every Essay Question. If your essay appears to have been completed on time, the grader matches the issues you discuss to the issues on the Grading Key. For each required issue, your rule statement and analysis are assessed for adequacy. If you discussed the required issue, your rule statement and analysis are adequate, and you gave some statement of conclusion, then you get the COVETED "70".

If the grader cannot find where you discussed required issues or rules easily, she will not waste her time looking for them. CLEARLY IDENTIFY THE ISSUES and RULES OF LAW.

Your answer must explain how the stated rule applies to the stated facts of the question. If no facts from the question are mentioned in your answer, the analysis will be deemed conclusionary and inadequate.

Your answer must state and adequately analyze all issues raised by the question. **An excellent analysis of one issue will NOT recover all of the points lost by failing to discuss another required issue.**

Bonus Points. Some essay answers are given bonus points. BONUS POINTS may be given for answers that cite ADDITIONAL RELEVANT ISSUES. Also, bonus points may be given for answers that are exceptionally WELL ORGANIZED and CITE CASES or UCC RULES.

Chapter 2: Identify the Area of Law

In the first year of law school Contracts classes may discuss the Restatement of Contracts, but they generally only test on two bodies of law, **Common Law of Contracts** and the **Uniform Commercial Code** (or this may be called "Sales"). That is all the California Bar tests.

In a law school examination it is not absolutely necessary to identify the area of law. But on Bar Examinations you must determine THE PROPER AREA OF LAW and TELL THE GRADER because your ability to properly determine the applicable law is an essential part of the examination. So state the applicable area of law as part of your essay answer.

The basic rule for determining the applicable law in a law school exam is to REMEMBER WHICH CLASS YOU ARE IN! Every year there is some clown that shows up for a mid-term or final on the wrong day, at the wrong time, prepared for the wrong examination.

The single most important rule in all law school and Bar Exams is READ THE CALL OF THE QUESTION! Failure to read and respond to the CALL of the question is the one, single most common reason law students fail.

In the excitement of the moment, you might misread the call of the question. So it is critical to remember which class you are in and CAREFULLY READ THE CALL.

In the first year of law school you will never have a "cross-over" question that mixes two areas of law. For example, in law school a CONTRACTS exam will not test you on TORTS. But the Bar Exams do have cross-over questions. NEVER answer the question with the wrong law.

PHRASE your answer properly. Remember defendants are only "GUILTY" of crimes. They are LIABLE for torts, not "guilty".

The party charged in a complaint is the DEFENDANT in all three areas of law -- contract, tort and criminal law. But only PLAINTIFFS bring actions based on tort or contract law. In criminal actions the complaint is brought by the PROSECUTION, not a victim or plaintiff.

On balance, it is a good, safe habit to start each essay with an affirmative statement of recognition concerning the area of law that applies to the question, and it never costs you.

Famous Last Words: *"This is the torts final, right?"*

Chapter 3: Outline Your Answer And COUNT THE ISSUES!

The second critical step in answering any essay question, after confirming the area of law, is to read the question and COUNT THE ISSUES to be discussed.

The issue outline is simply a list of the issues you will discuss, in the order you will discuss them. Make it "skeletal" in your own "personal shorthand." Don't waste time writing out detailed issue statements. Jot down **case names** and **special rules** like "Hadley v. Baxendale" and "Statute of Frauds." Jot down a few facts if you want, but DON'T WASTE TIME writing out every important fact.[2]

CONSIDER which issues you MUST discuss, which you MIGHT discuss and which are "unintended issues" that the grader does not want to hear about. Decide which issues are so minor, marginal, lacking in facts or attenuated that you should not discuss them. Look for specific wording in the question that indicates which issues are "required issues."

RE-READ THE FACTS to be sure you are not missing issues. Don't look so hard for hidden issues that you miss the issues that are obvious.[3]

Rewrite the outline as necessary, eliminating issues, or reordering issues. Usually you should list the issues in the same order they arise in the fact pattern, but there are exceptions. Try to list the issues in the same order they arise in the fact pattern, but there are exceptions.

SEPARATE THE ISSUES AND THE PARTIES discussing all rights, liabilities and remedies of each party in succession.

FOLLOW THE CALL. On a one-hour question outlining usually requires between 10 and 15 minutes. HOWEVER, if the call of the question actually lists the issues you are to discuss, then this outline process can (and must) be abbreviated. If the issues are listed for you, discuss all “sub-issues” that seem necessary and obvious but DO NOT DISCUSS ISSUES THAT ARE COMPLETELY IRRELEVANT TO THE CALL.

If the call of the question states the things to discuss, DISCUSS WHAT IT SAYS AND EVERYTHING DIRECTLY RELEVANT.[4]

> If the CALL says "what rights and remedies?" you MUST be sure to discuss the REMEDIES of the parties and not just the causes of action.
>
> If the CALL says, "what defenses might be raised?" you MUST discuss defenses as full issues.
>
> If the CALL describes A, B and C and then asks about the rights of B against C, DO NOT discuss A’s rights because the CALL only asks about the rights of B.

---

[2] Some people advocate copying all of the important facts from the essay question to the answer outline. That may help some students but to me it just seems a waste of time.

[3] This is a common error. Don’t look so hard for fleas you forget to talk about the elephant.

[4] Often you have to be sort of a “mind reader” to figure out what the professor wants to hear about.

READ SOME OF THE QUESTION, JUMP TO THE CALL, AND THEN READ AGAIN COMPLETELY. To properly outline an essay question,

FIRST read SOME of the facts, about ONE-THIRD of the fact pattern;
SECOND jump to the bottom of the question and determine the CALL;
THEN go back to the beginning and reread ALL of the facts.

As you read the question, draw lines to the margin and place symbols there designating the issues that might need to be discussed.

FOCUS ON THE AREA OF LAW. In law school you know what the area of law will be. But in a Bar Exam setting you have to figure out what area of law determines the outcome. So if the question is a common law contract question -- write a big "K" at the top of the page with a circle around it to reinforce in your mind that the area of law is common law CONTRACTS. For a UCC question write "UCC".

After you have read the question completely LIST AND NUMBER THE ISSUES on the bottom of the question sheet or on a separate piece of paper. Generally you should **list the issues in the order they appear in the question**, because that is usually the order of the Grading Key.

COUNT the issues! You should have between 5 and 12 issues. A question with less than 5 issues is highly suspicious -- you probably missed something big. It is almost impossible for an exam to produce proper results if there are fewer than 5 main issues. Often the issues are the defenses rather than the offenses. Defenses may be issues by themselves that require thorough analysis. The essay usually takes ONE HOUR to complete, and if you don't see enough to keep you busy for the time allotted you are probably missing some issues.

A question with more than 8 major issues is a racehorse exam where you have little time to analyze the issues in depth in a one-hour period. If you have more than 8 major issues, carefully consider whether some of them are "non-issues." A non-issue is something that the grader does not want to hear about. Those are discussed in more detail later.

If there are 8 legitimate issues you should plan on spending FIVE MINUTES on each in a one-hour exam.

If there are 12 issues to discuss you will only have 3 or 4 minutes to discuss each, and you will have to move very fast. Consider addressing some minor issues merely as "comments" in passing.

READ THE CALL AGAIN. Before you start writing, READ THE CALL OF THE QUESTION ONE MORE TIME and make sure your outline addresses the call.

Example: The example below shows a question (Question 1) about a contract dispute over the rental of a house and how you might mark up the question as you read it.

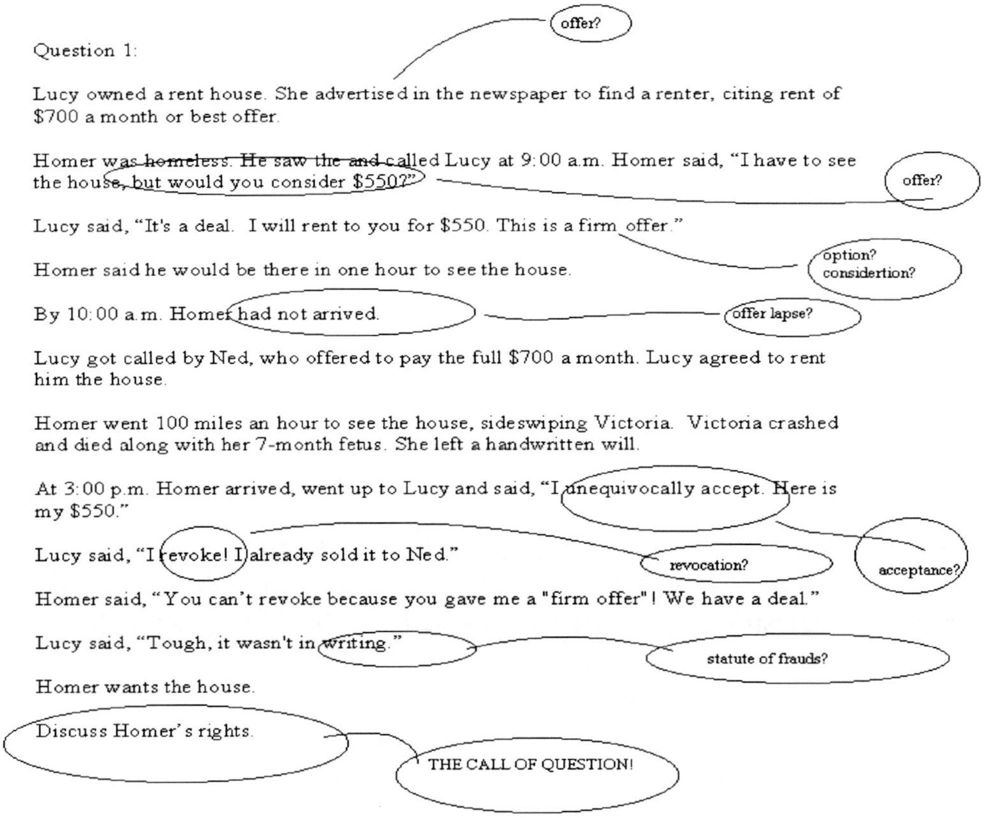
Question 1:

Lucy owned a rent house. She advertised in the newspaper to find a renter, citing rent of $700 a month or best offer.

Homer ~~was homeless. He saw the and~~ called Lucy at 9:00 a.m. Homer said, "I have to see the house, but would you consider $550?"

Lucy said, "It's a deal. I will rent to you for $550. This is a firm offer."

Homer said he would be there in one hour to see the house.

By 10:00 a.m. Homer had not arrived.

Lucy got called by Ned, who offered to pay the full $700 a month. Lucy agreed to rent him the house.

Homer went 100 miles an hour to see the house, sideswiping Victoria. Victoria crashed and died along with her 7-month fetus. She left a handwritten will.

At 3:00 p.m. Homer arrived, went up to Lucy and said, "I unequivocally accept. Here is my $550."

Lucy said, "I revoke! I already sold it to Ned."

Homer said, "You can't revoke because you gave me a "firm offer"! We have a deal."

Lucy said, "Tough, it wasn't in writing."

Homer wants the house.

Discuss Homer's rights.

Following this mark-up on the question itself, you should create a skeletal outline as shown below:

EXAMPLE QUESTION OUTLINE

Start -- with general CONTRACT statement -- define contract and elements.

1. Choice of law -- UCC (GOODS?) or common law? "house"
2. Does STATUTE OF FRAUDS apply, and is it satisfied? "house" = "land"
3. Was the ADVERTISEMENT an OFFER -- define OFFER.
4. Did H make OFFER at 9:00? "had to see it first".
5. Did L give H a VALID OPTION at 9:00? -- define OPTION, CONSIDERATION. "firm offer"?
6. Did H make valid ACCEPTANCE at 3:00? -- define ACCEPTANCE. Did offer LAPSE? REVOCATION -- not if offer lapsed.

Your outline should not be much more than shown here. But THINK IT THROUGH! Writing out an extensive outline with every fact, name, date, etc. is a big waste of time. Your outline should just list the ISSUES in the order you will discuss them, not all the facts. The facts are already listed in the question itself, so why repeat them? But THINK HARD about WHAT the facts suggest the issues the EXAMINER wants you to write about.

Chapter 4: Spotting Contract and UCC Issues

Since you lose points for every required issue you fail to discuss, it is CRITICAL TO SPOT all of the issues. BUT DON'T waste time discussing issues that do not really exist. This is easier said than done and introduces a certain level of sadism peculiar to law school.

The examiner wants you to discuss certain required issues. But question writers fall into two basic schools. The first, rational school, simply states the issues to be discussed in the call of the question. The second, less rational and often sadistic school of question writers uses only hints about the intended issues. Sometimes the "hints" are rather obvious. Other times they are so subtle the student has to be a psychic. At this extreme this approach is called HIDING THE BALL, and it is the stuff of law school horror stories.

The HIDE THE BALL question utilizes words and fact patterns that only vaguely suggest issues. This is like a code language known only to law school professors. The following is a list of "code" words and facts that are often used to indicate intended issues.

CONTRACTS Issue Spotting Hints

Issue Area and Coded Hint:	**Intended Issue:**
FORMATION ISSUES:	
1. Order from Advertisement/Catalogue:	Is the advertisement an offer?
2. Claim of reward, prize, bounty:	Is it a general offer validly accepted?
3. Do something (build, paint, etc.):	Unilateral contract?
4. Silently begin performance:	Acceptance of unilateral offer by performance?
5. Price/quantity inquiry?	Is this an offer?
6. Performance with silence:	Implied contracts?
7. Oral/telephone/verbally/said:	Is Statute of Frauds satisfied?
8. A "year":	Statute of Frauds?
9. Quantities with prices:	Statute of Frauds? UCC?
10. Special made goods:	UCC 2-201?
11. Lost writings:	Statute of Frauds?
12. A promise to pay debt of other:	Statute of Frauds? Main-purpose rule?
13. Accepted later:	Offer lapse?
14. Accepts in an hour/day/week:	Offer lapse?
15. "Ok, but...":	Rejection and counteroffer?
16. If I feel like it, decide to, want, etc.:	Illusory promise? Lack of consideration?
17. Accepted, then changed mind:	Mail box rules
18. Rejected, then changed mind:	Mail box rules
19. Sent offer/acceptance/rejection:	Mail box rules
20. Fax communication:	Sufficient UCC writing?
21. Hobby/enthusiast/fan:	Is he a merchant?
22. Only bought, never sold goods:	Is he a merchant?
23. Revocation before end of performance:	Saving doctrines of unilateral contracts?
24. Acceptance with different terms:	Mirror Image Rule? UCC 2-207?
25. Shipped wrong product:	Acceptance under UCC rule?
26. Building code violations:	Illegality of contract?
27. Illegal contracts:	In Pari Delicto?
28. Mistake/Misunderstanding:	Mutual misunderstanding? Peerless case.
29. Ambiguous offer/acceptance:	Objective theory of intent
30. Young, crazy, drunk:	Infancy? Incompetence?

31. Deceit, concealment:	Rescission?
MODIFICATION ISSUES:	
32. Modification - not goods:	Was consideration provided? Pre-existing duty?
33. Modification/later agreement - goods:	UCC modification by consent?
34. Modification with increase in $$$	Statute of Frauds?
35. Modification after assignment:	Effect of UCC 9-318 on secured transactions?
INTERPRETATION OF TERMS:	
36. More than one paper:	Integration?
37. Other agreements:	Parol Evidence Rule? Four-Corners?
38. Prior dealings:	Course of dealing? Past practices?
39. Ambiguous words:	Plain meaning?
THIRD-PARTIES/ ASSIGNMENT:	
40. Three parties?	Third party beneficiaries? Assignment?
41. Children, students, patients, tenants:	Intended third-party beneficiaries?
42. Funding agreement:	Proper expression of assignment?
43. World famous architect, artist:	Proper delegation subject matter?
44. Personal services, massage:	Proper delegation subject matter?
45. Covenants regarding future assignees:	Standing of assignee per UCC 9-206?
BREACH ISSUES:	
46. Performance doubts, insolvency:	Anticipatory Breach?
47. Assurances:	UCC Reasonable Assurances?
48. Unexpected conditions, death:	Impossibility? Impracticality? Mistake?
49. Unexpected difficulties:	Frustration of purpose? Impracticality?
50. Cancellation clauses:	Liquidated damage clauses? Unforeseeable?
51. Seller shipped wrong product:	Buyer's remedies? Cover? Reject? Keep?
52. Failure to act/protect:	Good faith and fair dealing? Duty to act?
53. Multiple shipments:	Divisible UCC contract?
54. Ambiguous grumbling:	Clear Anticipatory Breach or not?
REMEDY ISSUES:	
55. "Rights and remedies":	Buyer's/Seller's Remedies?
56. Breaching party partially performs:	Quantum Meruit?
57. Non-breaching party fails to act:	Failure to mitigate damages?
58. Land, works of art, etc.:	Specific performance?
59. Personal Services?	No specific performance?
60. Repairs:	Costs limited to fair market value?
61. Sentimental value:	Objective sentimental valuation?
62. Promise, reasonable reliance:	Estoppel?
63. Shipment of non-conforming goods:	Accommodation? Time to cure?
64. Lost profits?	Consequential damages? Hadley v. Baxendale
DEFENSES:	
65. Transfer to an innocent party:	Bone fide purchaser for value?
66. Forced to agree/Unfair:	Adhesion? Unconscionability? Coercion?
67. Young party:	Infancy? Voidable? Ratification?
68. Reliance, Misled:	Estoppel? Detrimental reliance?
69. Illegality:	Defense of illegality?
70. Elderly victim:	Defense of undue influence?
71. Check tendered as "payment in full"	Accord and satisfaction? UCC 3-311?

ISSUE SPOTTING EXAMPLES:

Example 1: *"Al and Bob had an oral contract that Al was to build a house for Bob. Bob agreed to pay Al when he gave him proof that all workmen and suppliers that had lien rights against the job had been properly paid.*

To make his payroll Al entered into a separate agreement with Carl. Carl agreed to advance Al the money to pay his workmen and suppliers each week. Al agreed that when Bob paid him he would reimburse Carl. The agreement said, "The Al-Bob contract is security for this agreement."

Al gave Bob proof his workmen and material suppliers had been paid, but Bob refused to pay Al unless he could prove he paid his ex-wife child support. Bob was adamant.

Al would not give Bob any proof he paid his child support and Bob never paid him. But Al kept building the house and demanded continued funding from Carl.

What are Carl's rights against Bob? Against Al?"

Issues: 1) WHAT LAW? Not <u>sale</u> of goods, but is secured transaction under UCC-9.

2) STATUTE OF FRAUDS. "oral" agreement. "Hints" discussion.

3) ASSIGNMENT? Carl is third party. Assigned rights under Al-Bob contract? Al-Carl contract creates security interest per UCC-9-102.

4) THIRD PARTY BENEFICIARY. Carl is a third party. Not intended.

5) BREACH by Al. Implied condition of Al-Carl contract -- Al will act to get payment from Bob. Al fails to act – breaches implied condition of Al-Carl contract.

6) REMEDY?

Example 2: *"Al ordered 60,000 campaign buttons by telephone from Sellco that said "Al for President." The purchase price was $.10 each, and Sellco said that if Al cancelled the order he would have to forfeit his deposit of $1000. Sellco ordered the buttons to be manufactured by Manco. The next day the Secretary of State told Al he would not be on the ballot because he failed to meet a filing deadline. Al immediately tried to cancel the order, but Sellco refused to accept or return his phone calls. Two weeks later Manco delivered the campaign buttons and billed Sellco. Sellco is demanding an additional $5,000. Al wants his $1000 deposit back. Discuss."*

Issues: 1) WHAT LAW? UCC – <u>contract for sale</u> of <u>movable</u> goods -- buttons.

2) MERCHANTS? Al not a merchant.

3) NEED FOR WRITING? No. Over $5000, but CUSTOM MADE goods.

4) FRUSTRATION OF PURPOSE. Purpose of contract is political campaign and all parties knew it.

4) LIQUIDATED DAMAGES. Reasonable?.

5) FAILURE TO MITIGATE. Sellco had a duty to cancel the Manco order and did not do so. They lose. Al gets all $1000 back?

Famous Last Words: *"That was really easy. I got done early. "*

Chapter 5: Non-Issues, Red Herrings and Splits

It is almost as disastrous to waste time discussing a non-issue as it is to fail to discuss an intended issue. It wastes time and irritates the grader.

Remember, you usually get ZERO POINTS for discussing any issue that is not on the Grading Key. The Bar examiner has little authority to give you points for imagination and inventiveness.

Also remember that while you discuss the non-issue, everyone around you is discussing the intended issues. They are making points and you are being stupid.

How to Recognize Non-Issues.

A non-issue is an issue that is not on the Grading Key. For every issue the grader wants you to discuss there will be one or more specific facts as "signs", "hints" or indicators. The grader does not want to be accused of "hiding the ball", so If you see a "really subtle" issue or an issue that you think "most people" will not recognize, that it is probably because it is an UNINTENDED ISSUE.

Hints. If the grader does not want you to discuss an issue, they may add HINTING WORDS to show that issue is irrelevant.

> **Example:** If the question says there was a "written contract" DO NOT waste time discussing whether the Statute of Frauds is satisfied.
>
> **Example:** If the question says the parties "entered into a contract" or "had an agreement" then the question is telling you not to waste time discussing "formation". Instead it is probably a <u>modification</u>, <u>breach</u>, <u>remedy</u> or <u>interpretation</u> question. DO NO waste time discussing whether or not there was an offer, acceptance and consideration.
>
> **Example:** If the question says the parties had a "valid" contract, DO NOT waste time discussing whether they had a valid contract or not.

Follow The Call.

Another way the examiner will direct you is by the CALL OF THE QUESTION. If the CALL is "structured" with a list of questions, the examiner is telling you the specific questions you are to address.

How Many Issues?

Another indicator is the NUMBER of clearly indicated issues. If you can count 6 to 8 clearly obvious issues to discuss, it is unlikely you are expected to discuss some other hidden and marginal issue.

Stay mainstream. Discuss only **mainstream law school issues**, not marginal or tangential issues of law. You may know something about the law from your own personal experience but <u>leave that knowledge at home</u> and only use knowledge you have been taught in law school.

Red Herrings.

Although the examiner will give you hints about the issues you are intended to discuss, she may also deliberately throw out a few RED HERRINGS to mislead the careless. A RED HERRING is a fact that hints at a totally different AREA OF LAW from the call of the question. The purpose of the Red Herring is to test your ability to focus on the CALL of the question without being distracted to irrelevant issues.

Example of a Red Herring. Suppose the question states:

> *"Tom sold a car to Dick for $1,000, and Dick promised to pay at the end of the month.*
>
> *Dick used the car to rob a bank, and Tom was a witness. The next day, while still fleeing from his crime, he negligently rammed the car into the back of Paula's car. Paula was Tom's casual friend and she died and left Blackacre to Harry, Tom's brother, by an attested will that was only signed by one witness, Tom. When Harry received the inheritance he was married to Wanda but he lived in California, and she had temporarily moved to Nevada to file for a quickie divorce in District Court so she could marry her lover, Tom.*
>
> *Dick didn't pay Tom. What are Tom's remedies?*

Here the call of the question is to discuss Tom's remedies against Dick. The only possible remedies Tom could have are under contract or tort law. Tom cannot "prosecute" Dick for his criminal acts. That might make Tom feel better, but it is not going to put money in his pocket. Here Tom has suffered no torts from Dick. Therefore, his only injury is the result of Dick's failure to pay $1,000 for the car. That is a contract action, and none of the other facts give Tom any cause of action in tort.

Tom's only cause of action is based on CONTRACT. Everything in the second paragraph is a Red Herring because it has absolutely nothing to do with contract law and would have no relevance to Tom's remedies against Dick.

Avoid Detailed Split Discussions Unless Called For.

A split is a conflict of rules. Some law school professors obsess on them, and some law students get obsessed about learning all of their intricate little nuances. Get a life. This is a waste of time and very distracting. Splits should always be mentioned in your rule statement, but discussion should be limited unless an in-depth analysis is clearly called for.

For example, States or Courts may differ on the law applied to certain issues. In stating the rule of law, it is important to say, "States are split on this issue," but usually little more needs to be said. AVOID GETTING HUNG UP ON DISCUSSION OF SPLITS.

Where the grader INTENDS for you to analyze a split of law, the question will clearly INDICATE that intent. In that case you should define each of the positions that have been taken, and whether a particular approach is considered the majority or minority view.[5]

---

[5] The concept of "majority" and "minority" is rather illogical. Law is not a matter of majority rule.

Example of a Split Approach. Suppose the question states:

> *Connie Conman, a first-year law student, told Sally Sucker, "I will pay you $1,000 if you will completely paint my house. I don't want just a promise to paint it. You can only accept this offer by actually painting it." Sally immediately started painting. After several days of effort, when she was all done except for one more brush stroke, Connie shouted, "I revoke!" Connie refused to let Sally finish the house with that one last brush stroke, and she refuses to pay Sally anything at all. What are Sally's rights and remedies?*

This question clearly calls for a discussion of the quirk in the common law that allowed an offeror to revoke his offer of a unilateral contract after the offeree had begun performance, but before completion of performance.[6] The better approach to this question is as follows:

> ***GOOD:*** *1. REVOCATION OF UNILATERAL OFFER?*
>
> *Under contract law a unilateral offer is one that by its own terms can only be accepted by complete performance. The common law allowed the unilateral contract offeror to revoke his offer at any time prior to acceptance by the offeree. This often produced an unjust situation in which an offeror could induce extensive effort by the offeree only to revoke his offer at the last moment.*
>
> *Modernly courts have devised SAVING DOCTRINES to stop the offeror of a unilateral contract from revoking his offer after becoming aware that the offeree has begun performance. Courts are split on the exact rationale for these saving doctrines, but the practical application is the same.*
>
> *The modern rule generally is that the offeror of a unilateral contract is ESTOPPED from revoking a unilateral contract offer for a reasonable period of time once they become aware the offeree has begun performance. Under an alternative approach the offeror can revoke the offer but must pay the offeree for the services rendered.*
>
> *Here Connie was the offeror of a unilateral contract because her offer to "pay $1,000" was conditioned upon the completion of the painting. Sally began performance because she "immediately started painting", and Connie was aware of this because she observed Sally painting.*
>
> *Therefore, under the modern approaches Sally would be given a reasonable period of time in which to complete performance with the one last brush stroke, and Connie would be estopped from revoking her offer until Sally was given that opportunity.*

---

[6] Note that the Courts generally abhor unilateral contracts and will find a contract to be bilateral unless the offer expressly and unequivocally indicates, as illustrated here, that ONLY a unilateral contract is intended.

The following approach goes into much more detail. It is a great answer, but it uses much more time and does not add much more value. Certainly there is no need to go into such details. There is also a good chance that you would get the four approaches confused and muddled anyway:

TOO DETAILED AND OBSESSED WITH THE SPLIT:

1. ISSUE -- Does Sally have a right to a reasonable amount of time to COMPLETE PERFORMANCE OF THE UNILATERAL CONTRACT?

Under the common law a unilateral contract offer is one that by its own terms can only be accepted by complete performance of the contract. But the common law allowed the unilateral contract offeror to revoke his offer at any time prior to acceptance by the offeree. This contradiction produced an unjust situation in which an offeror could induce extensive effort by the offeree only to revoke his offer at the last moment.

Modernly courts have devised four different SAVING DOCTRINES to stop the offeror of a unilateral contract from revoking his offer after becoming aware that the offeree has begun performance. The facts do not state where these events took place.

Under the Restatement 90 view the offeree converts the unilateral offer into an "option contract" that the offeree cannot revoke when he starts performance. Here Sally started performance when she started painting, so under this view he has an option contract that Connie cannot revoke, although Sally could abandon the project if she wants under this view.

Many States follow a different approach that holds that the offeree converts the unilateral offer ipso facto into a bilateral contract by beginning performance. Here Sally started performance, so if this State followed this approach this would have created a bilateral contract. In this case Connie could not revoke, and Sally would be obligated to complete performance of the last bush stroke.

Another view is the Estoppel View. In those jurisdictions the offeree is estopped from revoking once the offeree begins performance. Under this view Connie cannot revoke, but Sally is not obligated to perform the last brush stroke.

Under the fourth view, called the Quantum Meruit View, the offeror CAN revoke the offer, but the court will give the offeree Quantum Meruit reimbursement for the reasonable value of service and materials provided by the offeree prior to the revocation. Under this rule Sally would not be allowed to finish painting, and she may be given less than the $1,000 that Connie promised him.

Whether Sally could finish the painting and get the full $1,000 depends on the jurisdiction she is in.

There is nothing "wrong" with this last answer, and it is more thorough. But it is much longer and more time consuming without adding an equal amount of point value.

Famous Last Words: *"I couldn't remember which was the majority view."*

Chapter 6: A WARNING about Example Answers

You may see "exemplary" answers distributed by the California Bar. These answers can be very misleading and produce unfortunate results.

Some "example" answers are actually very bad answers because they are too long, too complex and took the student too much time to write.

Test this for yourself. Select one of the longer example answers and try to physically copy it in written form in the time allowed. Often this cannot be done. And if you cannot even copy the answer in the time allowed, you certainly could not read, outline, compose and write that same answer in the allotted time.

In fact, this is why many "brilliant" students fail in law school. They learn everything there is to know, attempt to say it all on the exam and run out of time before they can say it all.

Your goal should NOT be to tell everything there is to say about a subject. Your goal SHOULD BE to know everything necessary and to say everything that needs to be said and can be said in the time allotted.

Writing ONE excellent essay answer SHOULD NOT be your goal if it causes you to run out of time on the other questions. RATHER your goal should be to write ONE GOOD essay answer for each essay question asked within the given time limits.

The best answers are those that 1) state all required issues, 2) give correct rules of law for each, 3) give a straightforward analysis, 4) match the stated facts to the elements, and 5) state a simple conclusion, **all within the time allowed**.

The example answers given in this book are deliberately not perfect. They do not cite a lot of case law, and they do not go into a lot of detail. But they are feasible, adequate answers that can be outlined and written within a one-hour timeframe. [7]

Famous Last Words: *"I got a 90 on the first question, but..."*

---

[7] Since this book was first published many student's answers using the "nailing the elements" approach advocated here have actually been picked as "exemplary answers" on both the California FYLSX and also on the California General Bar Exam.

Chapter 7: Essay Time Budgeting Mechanics

Doing a proper essay is like doing comedy. Timing is as important as the material.

IT IS ABSOLUTELY ESSENTIAL to keep on schedule while writing essays. You must establish and stick to a time budget. Do not go overtime on one essay thinking you will catch up later on another -- you won't.

YOU MUST HAVE A WATCH OR CLOCK with you. Do not depend on the clock on the wall when taking an exam because it will not be set to the hour at the beginning of the test, it may not be easily visible, and it might stop working. One time I was taking an exam and the clock fell off the wall and smashed on the floor!

Set your watch or clock exactly to the hour (e.g. 9:00 a.m.) When the proctor says, "You may begin," start the clock!

The key to keeping your essay on schedule is to **NUMBER THE ISSUES** on your outline, **COUNT THE ISSUES** and **MARK YOUR OUTLINE** with the time each issue should be finished.

RESERVE 5 MINUTES at the end of each essay to underline issue statements and key words and to check for omissions. Therefore, if you spend 15 minutes outlining, and save 5 minutes at the end, you really have only 40 minutes to write.

> **Example.** Suppose it takes 15 minutes to read the question and create the Question Outline that was created in Chapter 3 above. There are 45 minutes left and 7 issues to write about (the beginning "contract statement" is like an issue). If you reserve 5 minutes at the end to underline and check your work, you have to write the 7 issues in 40 minutes. This gives you between 5 and 6 minutes to write about each issue.

FOLLOW THE PLAN -- MARK THE START/FINISH TIMES for each issue on the outline by adding 5 and 6 minutes (alternating) to the outline. Suppose the question in Chapter 3 above was the first essay of the morning, at 9:00 a.m. Marking the times for each issue on the outline, alternating 5 and 6 minute schedules, produces the following schedule:

QUESTION OUTLINE WITH TIME BUDGET

Homer v. Lucy

[9:15] Contract statement -- CONTRACT LAW, define contract and elements.

[:20] 1. Choice of law -- UCC (GOODS?) or common law? "house"

[:26] 2. Does STATUTE OF FRAUDS apply, and is it satisfied? "house" = "land"

[:31] 3. Was the ADVERTISEMENT an OFFER -- define OFFER.

[:37] 4. Did H make OFFER at 9:00? "had to see it first".

[:42] 5. Did L give H a VALID OPTION at 9:00? -- define OPTION, CONSIDERATION. "firm offer"?

[:48] 6. Did H make valid ACCEPTANCE at 3:00? -- define ACCEPTANCE, LAPSE -- hours late. REVOCATION -- not if offer lapsed.

STICK TO SCHEDULE. It does absolutely no good to develop a time schedule if it is not followed.

Check the schedule against the clock as you finish each issue of the essay. If you are behind schedule, shorten the analysis of the next issues to get back on schedule. If you are ahead of schedule, give more extensive rule statements, analysis and citation of facts in the remaining issues to use the extra time you have.

PRACTICE CHECKING THE CLOCK at the end of each issue in practice exams. This has to be practiced until it becomes a regular habit.

MODIFY to meet your personal needs AFTER you are proficient in this approach. You can relax your approach and may be able to eliminate the timing from the outline altogether eventually. But start out with a timed approach first to develop a "feel" for how much time to spend on each issue.

> ***Famous Last Words:*** *"I nailed the first one. It was exactly what I studied, and I did a whole blue book on it. But that last one was a real race horse. There just wasn't enough time."*

Chapter 8: Organizing the Answer

STATE THE PARTIES! First, present a heading stating the parties to the contract dispute, plaintiff first and defendant second as follows:

<u>Buyer v. Seller</u>

If there are two or more plaintiffs, or two or more defendants, analyze the rights, liabilities and defenses of one pair first.[8] Then after you have concluded the issues for the first pair present a new caption for the second plaintiff-defendant pair and discuss the issues that pertain to them:

<u>Promisee v. Assignee</u>

Once you state the parties (e.g. Promisee v. Assignee) discuss all issues and defenses between those two parties and don't restate these same parties switching their names around backwards.

NEVER try analyzing two defendants at the same time like this: "Buyer v. Seller and Manufacturer"

Usually it is best to discuss the various parties in the order in which they appear in the fact-pattern, but if they have alphabetical names (e.g. Adam, Bob and Charley) you might consider discussing them in that order.

INTRODUCTORY STATEMENT. Second, for <u>contracts questions only</u> an introductory statement is a good idea because it allows you to define the term "contract" at the very beginning of the essay.

> *"The rights and remedies of the parties depend on whether they had a valid contract. A contract is a promise or set of promises the performance of which the law will recognize as a duty and for the breach of which the law will provide a remedy."*

ORGANIZATION BY CALL STRUCTURE. If the call of the question is STRUCTURED, it indicates the organization of the answer, and you must follow that organization EXACTLY because the Grading Key will be in that precise form.

For example, if the question asks,

> *"Discuss the following issues:*
> a. *What remedies does W have against Y?*
> b. *Can W bring an action against X?*
> c. *What defenses can X raise?"*

[8] As might be the case where there is an assignment or delegation.

Then, discuss your issues within the order of this framework. For example, the structured call above may result in the following answer structure:

"*a. What remedies does W have against Y?*
1. *Consequential damages?*
2. *Restitution?*
3. *Specific Performance?*

b. Can W bring an action against X?
4. *Intended Third Party Beneficiary?*

c. What defenses can X raise?"
5. *Statute of Frauds?*
6. *Impossibility?*

GENERAL ORGANIZATION OF CONTRACT ANSWERS. Generally, except as noted below, if the call of the question is general, such as "Discuss," the organization of issues in your answer should follow the following general pattern.

1) Prefaced with a statement that defines a contract. The preface might also list the basic elements of a valid contract, but that is optional.
2) Next consider discussing whether the UCC applies or only common law. If the UCC applies, discuss whether the parties are MERCHANTS.
3) Next is a written contract required by the STATUTE OF FRAUDS or UCC?
4) At this point, determine what type of contract question you have. There are SIX BASIC TYPES OF CONTRACT QUESTIONS, but most questions combine these elements:

a) FORMATION	(Was a contract formed?),
b) TERMS	(What were the terms?),
c) THIRD PARTIES	(Who can enforce?),
d) BREACH	(Who breached first?),
e) DEFENSES, and	(What defenses can be raised?)
f) REMEDIES	(What remedies are available?)

If the question is a FORMATION or BREACH question your answer should go through all communications between the parties CHRONOLOGICALLY to determine if and when the contract formed and/or when the contract was breached.

If the TERMS are in dispute, common issues are: Which communication was the OFFER? Which was the ACCEPTANCE? Does the UCC apply? What terms were MATERIAL ALTERATIONS? Are the parties MERCHANTS? Was there an enforceable MODIFICATION? Was there was a WAIVER of a condition? Or was there an ACCORD AND SATISFACTION?

The question of THIRD PARTIES depends on whether there was communication of a valid ASSIGNMENT, DELEGATION, or if there was a communicated intention at the time of contract formation for benefits to flow to third parties.

Discuss each major DEFENSE as a separate issue. A common issue is whether there was a writing sufficient to satisfy the Statute of Frauds or UCC.

Usually REMEDIES should be discussed from the perspective of the non-breaching party but sometimes you have to discuss the remedy of the BUYER separately from the remedy of the SELLER. If the property is UNIQUE a party may demand SPECIFIC PERFORMANCE. If there would be unjust enrichment, a party may demand RESTITUTION (which might be called "quantum meruit" by your professor).

For example: If, "Able agreed to paint Baker's house by September 1 for $4,000, and then Able assigned the painting contract to Charley who did not finish the painting until October 1," the structure of the answer would be:

Introductory statement defining "contract."

Baker v. Able

1) Was TIME OF THE ESSENCE?[9]

2) Did Able effectively ASSIGN his rights under the contract?[10]

3) Did Able effectively DELEGATE his duties? Effect on his liability?

4) Was there a BREACH? Major or minor?

5) Baker's REMEDY?

Baker v. Charley

6) Does Baker have standing as a THIRD PARTY BENEFICIARY?[11]

7) Baker's REMEDY?

[9] Nothing indicates discussion of the UCC is called for so that issue is skipped. Further, it is clear this is not a "formation" question either. But tardy performance is a breach, so it is a good idea to discuss whether time was of the essence so you can easily conclude whether the breach is major or minor.

[10] Note that if someone who has a duty to perform "assigns" a contract two issues are raised – assignment and delegation.

[11] The third party beneficiary issue arises from every "delegation" because Baker is an intended third party beneficiary of the Able-Charley delegation contract.

Chapter 9: Stating the Issue

ISSUES: An "issue" is a legal or equitable claim, plea or defense (usually disputed or disputable) that can be settled by a single rule or definition of law that requires proof of a limited number of "legal elements".

Phrase the Issue for an EASY DETERMINATION. The best phrasing for the issue statement depends on the area of law: Set up your issue as a "straw man" so that you can easily "knock it down" by identifying the elements, showing the facts support the elements, and thereby go on to consider other issues. Avoid phrasing an issue in a way that forces you to a conclusion that necessarily precludes discussion of other necessary issues.

Issues should be narrow and not so overbroad they turn on several different rules of law.

Good Issues:

- Offer by Bob on May 1?
- Acceptance by Dick on 6/2?
- Parol Evidence Rule?
- Promissory estoppel?

Overbroad Issues:

- Rights of Bob?
- Valid contract?
- Defenses of Dick?
- Equitable relief?

Issues Structured by Call. If the question has a structured call, reflect that call in your answer with the "issues" organized to support that overall organization.

For example, if the question asks,

> *"Discuss the following issues:*
> *a. What are the rights and remedies of B?*
> *b. What defenses can A raise? "*

Your answer should be structured with the issues like this:

B v. A

a. Rights and Remedies of B
1. (first issue)
2. (second issue)

b. Defenses of A
3. (third issue)
4. (fourth issue)

General Issue Structure. Number issues with ARABIC numbers. And UNDERLINE the entire issue statement. The issue can either be written out like "Did Bob make an OFFER on May 1?" or they can be abbreviated to a single word like "OFFER?" Writing the main word in UPPER CASE brings it to the reader's attention.

Don't use Roman numerals or letters for issue statements because they waste time.

Use a question mark? The issue should be a disputed or disputable claim so mark it with a question mark (?).

Match Issue Numbers to Your Outline. The numbers on the issues should match the numbers on your outline. That helps prevent you from accidentally skipping an issue you intended to write about.

Examples:

1) *OFFER on 6/1?*
2) *STATUTE OF FRAUDS?*
3) *IMPOSSIBILITY?*

Phrase Issues for EASY ANSWERS. Phrase issue statements so they are easy to answer! Make the issue a "straw man" with clear elements that you can easily "knock down" by proving the elements.

Contracts Issues. In FORMATION and BREACH issues, always cite the communications CHRONOLOGICALLY, citing the time or date of each communication.

For REVOCATION the issue is whether it was an EFFECTIVE revocation before an acceptance took place.

For "firm offers" and MODIFICATION the issue is whether CONSIDERATION is necessary or adequate.

Contract Issue Examples:

1) *Was letter of 5/1 an OFFER?*
2) *Was letter of 6/1 an OFFER?*
3) *Was letter of 7/1 an ACCEPTANCE?*
4) *TERMS?*
5) *STATUTE OF FRAUDS require a writing?*
6) *modification supported by CONSIDERATION?*
7) *ANTICIPATORY BREACH?*
8) *failure to deliver on 9/1 a BREACH by Seller?*
9) *Duty to MITIGATE?*
10) *Did Seller have TIME TO CURE?*
11) *DAMAGES?*

Chapter 10: Nailing the Elements – The HEART of the Essay

The heart of every law school or FYLSX essay is the ANALYSIS, and the key to analysis is **NAILING THE ELEMENTS.** This means to

1) State an ISSUE raised,
2) Cite LEGAL AUTHORITY for a rule,
3) State the LEGAL RULE with clear **ELEMENTS** to be proven, and then
4) PROVE that **HERE** EACH and EVERY ELEMENT of the rule can be proven **BECAUSE** a relevant **SUPPORTING FACT** exists in the fact pattern.

A heart of NAILING THE ELEMENTS consists of 2 parts:

1) State the ELEMENTS of the RULE, and
2) NAIL (prove) each ELEMENT of the rule with a QUOTED FACT.

NAILING THE ELEMENTS is the easiest thing to do, and it produces the greatest benefit. Yet some students simply refuse to do it. Those students are usually referred to by other students in the past tense.

Follow This Order:

1) Cite the AUTHORITY.

This is mandatory on a Bar Exam and it is a good habit to start in law school. Show the grader that you know the area of law that applies. This is a good approach to citing a CASE (Peerless, etc.), a STATUTORY SCHEME (the UCC, etc.), or a LEGAL CONCEPT (Statute of Frauds, etc.). TELL THE GRADER THE LEGAL AUTHORITY your answer is based upon.

To do this, start your answer with the word "Under ..." and cite the authority for your rule of law.

Examples:

1) Under common law ...
2) Under contract law
3) Under Hadley v. Baxendale...
4) Under the Statute of Frauds ...
5) Under the UCC ...

2) State the LEGAL RULE.

Generally, you should state together all rules of law that apply to the issue FIRST in ONE SPOT. Do not "dribble" the rule out in bits and pieces here and there in the analysis.

The grader is looking for the RULE to follow the ISSUE. You must put the rule where the grader expects to find it. Follow the IRAC approach -- put the RULE right after the ISSUE.

Until you get familiar with this approach it is very beneficial to underline the rule elements that must be proven. You can stop doing this later after you have made "nailing the elements" a firm habit. But when you are first learning HOW TO WRITE exams, underlining the ELEMENTS in the rule will help you focus on WHAT YOU NEED TO PROVE.

Examples of Legal Rules with Elements Underlined:

1) *Under contract law an OFFER is a manifestation of present contractual intent sufficiently certain as to terms that an objective observer would reasonably believe assent would form a bargain.*
2) *Under the MIRROR IMAGE RULE of common law an acceptance was an unequivocal assent to the terms of an offer but under the UCC any offer not otherwise expressly conditioned may be accepted in any reasonable manner including a promise to ship or shipment of conforming or non-conforming goods.*
3) *Under the Statute of Frauds a contract for sale of LAND must be in WRITING.*

3) NAIL EACH ELEMENT OF THE RULE WITH A FACT. This is the single MOST COMMON REASON PEOPLE FAIL THE BAR.

Remember, IF YOU DO NOT NAIL, YOU WILL FAIL!

You must show that each ELEMENT is PROVEN BECAUSE there is a FACT provided to prove it. "Nail" each element with a fact from the question by using the following form:

"*Here* [the ELEMENT of law is PROVEN] *BECAUSE* "[some FACT is given]".[12]

Try to Use One "Because" for Each Element. Use the word "because" and give a "quoted fact" for each and every element in the rule. If the rule has four elements, there should be four "because"s and four "quoted facts".

You can combine two or more elements into a statement and otherwise modify this approach. But this general approach MUST be used.

If you follow this "Here ... because ... "quote"" approach, you will AUTOMATICALLY focus on each element of your rule and to the facts that prove that element.

4) Give a SIMPLE CONCLUSION.

This is the least common problem area. All students are too quick to cite conclusions. The simplest approach is to state, "Therefore..."

About the only error one can make in citing a conclusion is to be WIMPY or WISHY-WASHY.

---

[12] Avoid saying, "Here...Here...Here..." Instead, say something like, "Here...And...Also...Further..."

Skeleton of NAILING Approach Structure.

Your essay should have this skeletal form:

Explanation :	Written Structure :
[Numbered, underlined issue statement]	*1. [ISSUE as word, phrase or easy question]?*
[Cite Authority]	*Under* [Authority],
[State Rule with each Element underlined.]	[the Rule is ... with Element 1, Element 2, etc.]
[Address each Element by saying "Here..." The Element to be proven is underlined again. Then say "**because**" and quote a Fact to prove the element of the rule.]	*Here* [Element 1, underlined] *is proven/shown to be true* ***because*** ["Fact 1", Quoted].
[Repeat for each additional Element.]	*And* [Element 2, underlined] *is proven/shown to be true* ***because*** ["Fact 2", Quoted].
[Give a terse and definite Conclusion]	*Therefore,* [ISSUE is true/false.].

Example of Proper Analysis: If the question says,

"On January 1 Bob orally agreed to build a house for Owen on some land Owen had inherited from his father. The agreement said that Bob had to have the house completely finished by December 1. Bob did not get the house done until December 15. Can Bob raise the Statute of Frauds as a defense?"

Analyze as follows:

> "*Owen v. Bob*
>
> *1. STATUTE OF FRAUDS?*
> *Under the STATUTE OF FRAUDS a contract for conveyance of an interest in land must be in writing in order to be enforced.*
>
> *Here there was a contract without a writing because the parties "orally agreed." It was a contract for building a "house" but not for land because "Owen had inherited" the land.*
>
> *Therefore, the Statute of Frauds did not require a writing."*

An Example of a Bad Answer:

Bad essay answers are usually bad for a number of small reasons. Each of the little problems adds up to a big problem. Compare the bad answer below to the correct answer above.

> *"STATUTE OF FRAUDS:*
>
> *MY LEG = MARRIAGE, YEAR, LAND, EXECUTOR, GUARANTOR.*
>
> *Here Bob orally agreed to build a house for Owen on some land that Owen inherited from his father. Bob was to finish by December 1. He breached by not finishing the house until December 15.*
>
> *OFFER. An offer is a manifestation of willingness to contract. There must have been an offer since because Bob agreed to build a house.*
>
> *ACCEPTANCE. Under the common law an acceptance must be the mirror image. Here there clearly was an acceptance.*
>
> *CONSIDERATION. Consideration is an exchange of promises. Here Bob promised to build a house, but there are no facts about whether Owen promised anything.*
>
> *Bob would argue that this was LAND and he didn't breach since the contract was not in writing. Owen would say it was not for land, just for a <u>service</u> to build the house on the land he already owned.*
>
> *The law abhors a forfeiture, and the court would look to the intent of the parties.*
>
> *Therefore, Bob would not prevail."*

This answer is bad for a lot of reasons. Put yourself in the grader's place. Pretend it is late at night and you have already gone through about 80 bad essays. You are tired of seeing bad essays. You are in no mood to cut any slack. Here is how you might feel about this essay:

> *"Hurumph. Gives a <u>mnemonic</u> as being a rule of law. Then facts are restated. How many times does "because" appear? None. Then what is this old cliché about the law "abhorring a forfeiture"?*
>
> *The call of the question is about the statute of frauds but they start discussing formation.*
>
> *Not one fact quoted. Never says "because"."*

Famous Last Words: *"I used the facts because I rewrote them all!"*

Chapter 11: Don't Give "Conclusionary" Analysis

The "BAD ANSWER" in the previous chapter is conclusionary. Law students are often told their answer is "conclusionary" but that term is seldom explained. Sometimes the student is told to "use the facts." That also is seldom explained.

A "conclusionary" analysis is one that jumps to a conclusion regarding an issue without any analysis of the facts needed to prove the elements of the legal rule. The conclusion is unsupported by evidence.

The identifying characteristic of a conclusionary analysis is that the word "because" never appears BECAUSE no FACTS are referred to.

Example: Suppose the question says,

> "On January 1 Bob orally agreed to build a house for Owen on some land Owen had inherited from his father. The agreement said that Bob had to have the house completely finished by December 1. Bob did not get the house done until December 15. Can Bob raise the Statute of Frauds as a defense?"
>
> A **CONCLUSIONARY** answer is --
>
> *"1. STATUTE OF FRAUDS?*
> *Under the STATUTE OF FRAUDS contracts for conveyances of interests in land must be in writing to be enforceable.*
>
> *Here the contract is not for land.*
>
> *Therefore, Bob cannot use the statute of frauds as a defense.*

The conclusionary analysis jumps to a conclusion that the issue is proven by reference to the rule but without any reference to supporting facts.

Here you might argue there is some reference to the facts because the student writes that "the contract is not for land. But there is no reference to any fact that proves this assertion. The word "because" is missing. There is no explanation that the contract is not for land because Owen had already "inherited" the land and just wanted a house built on land he already owned.

In an essay there should be one "because" and at least one reference to the facts for every element of every rule. This rule can be relaxed after you have made “nailing the elements” a firm habit, but if there are few or no "because"s at all, and few references to the facts, the essay will become conclusionary and totally unacceptable.

Chapter 12: Don't "Restate Facts"

After law students are admonished to "use the facts" they are then chastised for "restating the facts". How can you "use the facts" without "restating the facts"? What does this mean?

The bad habit of "restating the facts" simply means that the student simply repeats the facts like a parrot without providing any analysis or explanation relating those facts to the elements of the rule that needs to be proven.

The identifying characteristic of an answer that simply restates facts is that the word "because" never appears BECAUSE no ELEMENTS are referred to.

An analysis which "simply restates facts" jumps to a conclusion that the issue is proven by reference to the facts without reference to the legal elements of the rule.

Example: Suppose the question says,

> "On January 1 Bob orally agreed to build a house for Owen on some land Owen had inherited from his father. The agreement said that Bob had to have the house completely finished by December 1. Bob did not get the house done until December 15. Can Bob raise the Statute of Frauds as a defense?"

An answer with **UNNECESSARY RESTATING OF FACTS** would be --

> *"1. STATUTE OF FRAUDS?*
> *Under the STATUTE OF FRAUDS contracts for interests in land must be in writing to be enforceable.*
>
> *Here Bob orally agreed on January 1 to build "a house" on some land that Owen had "inherited" from his father. The house had to be done by December 1 and Bob did not complete it until December 15.*
>
> *Therefore, Bob cannot use the statute of frauds as a defense.*

The problem with this answer is that it jumps to a conclusion by simply repeating all the facts, but it does not relate any particular ELEMENT of law to any particular fact.

For example, it says Bob agreed to build "a house" but it does not explain why that fact is important. The explanation, that this is not a sale of land because Bob was building on land that Owen already owned is absent from the answer.

If an answer refers to a lot of "facts" but never uses the word "because" then it is unacceptable.

Follow The Yellow Brick Road. The simple, mechanical way to improve essay analysis is to remember what Dorothy said when she went down the Yellow Brick Road in the Wizard of Oz -- "BECAUSE, BECAUSE, BECAUSE, BECAUSE, BECAUSE." If an answer refers to a lot of "facts" but never uses the word "because" then it is unacceptable.

Chapter 13: Avoid "Paddling "

Many law students use "analysis" composed of alternative arguments from each side of a dispute. This "sing-song" approach is referred to as "paddling" because it is like paddling a canoe, first arguing the position of one party, then switching to argue the position of the other side. This can be effective at times, but it is usually inferior to nailing the elements.

Example of a Paddling Answer: Suppose the question says,

> "On January 1 Bob orally agreed to build a house for Owen on some land Owen had inherited from his father. The agreement said that Bob had to have the house completely finished by December 1. Bob did not get the house done until December 15. Can Bob raise the Statute of Frauds as a defense?"
>
> An answer with a "Paddling" approach would be --
>
> *"1. STATUTE OF FRAUDS?*
> *Under the STATUTE OF FRAUDS contracts for conveyances of interests in land must be in writing to be enforceable.*
>
> *Bob would say the house he built became part of the land when he "fixed" it to the land. He would argue that the contract had to be in writing and was not. Owen would say that he already owned the land since he inherited it from his father.*
>
> *Therefore, Bob might be successful if the court holds that the house became part of the land when it was built.*

This "paddling" approach is not totally worthless, because it does focus on the facts and the elements of the rule. In fact, it is a good approach to follow when there is an element that is only supported by "arguable" facts. In that situation it provides a framework for explaining the strength and weakness of the supporting facts as viewed from each side. But it is simply overdone and often used where it is unnecessary.

Probably the worst thing about this approach is that it gets really irritating to the grader. It is like listening to children bicker.

Chapter 14: Test Taking Mechanics

It is incredible the weird and stupid things law students do at examinations. The following comments cover the simple mechanics of preparing for and writing an exam. These points seem obvious but they are the reasons a lot of people fail law school and the Bar Exams.

If you work, take three days off for all first-year law school exams! For strange unknown reasons beginning law students are the most overconfident people in the world. Take three full days to study for each first-year law school exam. This is especially true of the first mid-terms. The first-year mid-term exams are the most important exams you will ever take. If you fail one of those first exams, you will be in a hole, on probation and at risk of expulsion for all the rest of your law school experience.

Write at least eight timed exams. That means you should spend <u>at least 8 hours</u> just writing essay answers. You can only physically write for about 4 hours a day, so this means you need to spend about TWO DAYS writing exams, getting your timing down and memorizing what to say.

Learn the mnemonics. If you don't know the mnemonics like COALL, CCCC, etc. you are the creek without a paddle.

Outline your answer and follow your outline! It does you no good to outline an essay answer if you are not going to use it.

Bring decent pens. Whether you handwrite the essay or type it, buy a small box of good, smooth writing black ink pens. DO NOT write an essay exam with colored pens or gummy old ink pens that give you writer's cramp and leak all over. [I chided one student for using a crummy pen. He said he liked that pen. He just flunked the Bar for the fourth time.]

Bring a Watch or Clock. Bring one or more watches or clocks that you can adjust to the hour so you can time your work. Start it when they say, "begin".

Use paragraphs, and lots of them. The "stream of consciousness" approach to writing does not thrill the grader. I don't think e e cummings was an attorney. Break your answer up into paragraphs of between one and four sentences.

Leave lots of blank space. Leave extra space between paragraphs, at the bottom of the page, and between issues. Leave space so that if you forget to mention an issue you will have room to go back and insert it.

Never switch defendants (plaintiffs) in mid page. Start a new page.

Never start a new issue at the bottom of a page. Go to the top of the next page to begin a new issue. Don't be afraid to ask for and use a lot of paper.

Typewriter ribbons. Bring plenty of typewriter ribbons if you type.

Do the essays in order. If you are given three essays, do them in the order given. DO NOT think that you will improve your score by doing them out of order. It will NOT improve your score and it can cause a major disaster. For example, there can be a problem with the third question. If everyone but you is doing Question 1 the proctors might find an ambiguity on Question 3 and make a timely announcement. That would save the day for everyone -- but you!

Further, if you are working on the same question as everyone else, you can feel their anxiety and the pace of their work. You can feel when a question is easy or hard. You can feel yourself getting behind on the time.

Print out each page of the essay as it is completed! If you type on a word processor, DO NOT wait to the end of the essay to print it out. If you have a power failure, you will be screwed. Print each page as it is finished!

Do not underline with the typewriter. Most typewriters underline too slowly. Use ALL CAPS to identify words you feel are important and underline them manually with a pen after the page is finished. This gives you a timely chance to review your answer too.

Get some sleep. It is absolutely counter-productive to study all night before the exam.

Don't get wired. It is a bad strategy.

> ***Famous Last Words:*** *"I have to get to the airport. My wife and I are in a ballroom dancing tournament in L.A. and I have to be there by 5:00." (Actually stated immediately after a mid-term.)*

> ***Famous Last Words:*** *"I didn't actually write any timed essays, but I look at some of the old essay questions and understood them."*

> ***Famous Last Words:*** *"I think I'm ready. I crammed all night."*

> ***Famous Last Words:*** *"I did the third question first. It seemed easier."*

Chapter 15: Essay Answer Formats – WHAT to Say and HOW to Say It

Before you walk into a law school or Bar exam, you **MUST** be able to recite, verbatim, prepared responses to a wide variety of potential questions. If you don't have prepared responses memorized, you are dead. You will not have enough time to think up a good answer on the spot. You will get "brain lock", run out of time on your essay answers, panic and your goose will be cooked.

You MUST be able to recite, from memory, the definitions and rules of OFFER, ACCEPTANCE, and CONSIDERATION without hesitation or mental reservation. You MUST be able to state by memory some of the UCC statute NUMBERS. Cite *Hadley v. Baxendale* for a discussion of consequential damages.

Am I kidding? NO.

What if the professor says it is not necessary? Don't believe him. When the other students know it and you don't is he going to forgive you? NO.

Will any of the other students learn all this? YES. Will they tell you? NO, they will act like they don't know any more than you do.

How? You must develop this ability by repetition and practice. You must memorize and be prepared to recite a significant portion of the material presented in the following **Issues and Answers** if you are to succeed in passing your exams.

The following chapter provides you with **EVERY ISSUE, AUTHORITY, DEFINITION and RULE** of law you need to be prepared for most questions. You can fake anything else.

Important Stuff. As you read through the following issue and answer formats, you may be overwhelmed with the feeling that, "There ain't no way in Hell I can memorize all of this." This is a natural reaction. But some of the following is more important than the rest, and the important portions will be identified and marked for you like this → **Important!** As for the rest, you should at least be able to fake it.

How to Memorize. The way to memorize the important portions of the following is like memorizing the Gettysburg Address -- read it, recite into a tape recorder, and play it back against the text. Do it naked if you have to. Sing it if you have to. Just do it.

The Text Format Used Here. In the following issue and answer formats, the text you should know and be prepared to produce is presented in *italics*. Additional information, comments and notes are presented in plain text.

Fake the Rest. You can't memorize everything. You can't know everything. You are human. So just listen in class, read a course outline and fake anything that is not in this book. But KNOW the definitions and rules that this book says are **Important!**

Four Ploys to Save You on an Exam.

When you are taking law exams you will invariably find yourself in perplexing and difficult situations. Here are four ideas you can use to get yourself out of a tight spot.

1. **"Actions Imply Intentions."** If no facts expressly state what the parties' intentions were at the time they acted, their actions (or lack thereof) imply their intentions.

    For Example: You are presented with facts that don't expressly say what a defendant's intentions were at some point in time. You can say, "The defendant impliedly did not intend to steal at the time of the breaking because she did not take the TV until the next morning."

2. **"The Courts Have Often Been Split."** If you are presented with an issue that you have either never seen before or else you recall reading something about it but can't remember which way the Courts decided the issue, you can always say, "The Courts have been split on this issue..." It sounds very "lawyer-like" and it is always true. Then you should probably discuss the "balance rule" and "reasonableness" standards presented below.

3. **"The Court Would Balance."** For almost every issue in every area of law there is some sort of "balance test". In these "balance tests" the Court considers the interests of the parties, the plaintiff and defendant, the interests of the Court itself, the interests of third parties, and the public interest. So if you don't know what the law is or what to say consider saying, "The Court would balance the interests of the parties in light of the public interest and the Court's own interest considering the impact on the efficient administration of justice." This sounds good, and you can make it up on the spur of the moment.

4. **"Reasonable expectations...reasonable behavior...reasonable person..."** For virtually every issue in every area of law the rule of law is based on what is "reasonable". Sometimes it is "reasonable expectations", sometimes "reasonable behavior", sometimes "reasonably foreseeable, and sometimes "reasonable person". But it is always "reasonable". So if you use the word "reasonable" liberally in describing the rule of law and the considerations of all concerned, you usually cannot go wrong.

    For Example: Putting this all together, suppose you are presented with some dispute that raises an issue that you have never seen before and don't know the law at all. You have to fake it. A good approach is to say, "The Courts have been split on this issue. The Court would balance the interests of the parties in light of the public interest and the Court's own interest considering the impact on the efficient administration of justice. The decision would depend on the reasonable expectations of each party in light of the reasonable needs of third parties and the impact on the Court. Here the reasonable expectation of .... And a reasonable person would believe... And it was reasonably foreseeable that... Therefore..."

Chapter 16: Answering Contract and UCC Questions

There are several basic types of contract essay questions. These types are often combined, and some issues can be skipped in some questions that do not call for their discussion. Some people recognize 4 basic contract question formats, but in this book I recognize 6 basic types:

1) **FORMATION QUESTIONS** – Raise issues of whether contract ever formed at all.
   Was there an OFFER?
   ACCEPTANCE?
   Manifestation of INTENT?
   Was the contract for a LEGAL PURPOSE?
   Supported by CONSIDERATION? [Seldom an issue on a UCC question!]
   Between parties with LEGAL CAPACITY?

2) **TERMS DISPUTES** -- What were the terms of the contract?
   Sufficiently CERTAIN that a court can enforce?
   Was there a MODIFICATION supported by consideration?
   Is a term or promised performance a MATERIAL CONDITION?
   Is a given term or promise INCLUDED or EXCLUDED from the agreement?

3) **THIRD PARTY QUESTIONS** -- Who has the right to bring an action?
   Were there THIRD-PARTY BENEFICIARIES?
   Was there a VALID ASSIGNMENT?
   Was there a VALID DELEGATION?

4) **DEFENSE QUESTIONS** – Focus on defense issues.
   Statute of Frauds satisfied?
   Lack of consideration?
   Illegal purpose?
   Rights of underage party?
   Fraud? Duress?

5) **BREACH QUESTIONS** – Focus on the issue of who breached first?
   Anticipatory breach?
   Major or Minor breach?
   Waiver?

6) **REMEDY QUESTIONS** – Raise issues of what each party can recover and how.
   SPECIFIC PERFORMANCE?
   RESTITUTION (quantum meruit concepts)?
   RIGHT TO CURE?
   COVER?
   FAILURE TO MITIGATE?
   ESTOPPEL?
   SAVING DOCTRINES?

What NOT to Discuss.

If the contract question says, "Bob and Joe had a contract," DO NOT discuss whether or not Bob and Joe had a contract. Obviously they had a contract, because the facts just told you they had a contract.

If the question says there was a contract, it is a BREACH or REMEDY question and NOT a FORMATION question. So don't waste time discussing formation non-issues in these situations.

What TO discuss.

On the other hand, if there are a lot of questions back and forth about, "Will you take this?" and "Maybe I would accept that," then it is a FORMATION question that needs discussion of OFFER, ACCEPTANCE and so forth.

If the question says "oral agreement" then the STATUTE OF FRAUDS is a suggested issue. Conversely if the question says there was a "detailed written contract" the PAROL EVIDENCE RULE is suggested. [13]

Simply put, look at the facts presented as clues as to what you are to discuss and what not.

Mnemonics for Contracts Essays:

- **COALL** = The required elements of a valid contract -- Consideration, Offer, Acceptance, Legal capacity, Legal purpose.
- **MYLEG** = Contracts that require a writing -- Marriage, over a Year, Land, Executors of estates, Guarantors of debts. [14]
- **CCCC** = Consequential Damages -- Contemplated at formation, Certain in amount, Caused by breach, Couldn't be avoided.
- **DAM FOIL** = Parol Evidence Rule exceptions -- Duress, Ambiguity, Mistake, Fraud, Oral condition precedent, Illegality, Lack of consideration.

Why are These Important? Remembering these mnemonics helps you keep a mental checklist of things that might be ISSUES to discuss.

What is the application of UCC Article 2? UCC Article 2 governs <u>contracts for the sale of goods.</u>

What is a GOOD? A "good" is anything movable at the time of identification to a contract. [15] What does this mean? It means that if you can MOVE IT when you can IDENTIFY it to the contract. The UCC requires a writing for a <u>sale</u> of <u>goods</u> worth <u>more</u> than $500. [16]

---

[13] The Statute of Frauds and Parol Evidence Rule are like flip sides of a coin. If one is an issue the other cannot be an issue at all.

[14] Modernly UCC 2-201 governs contracts for the sale of goods, not the Statute of Frauds.

[15] Including special made goods, standing crops and timber, unborn animals, and minerals in the ground to be removed by the seller (e.g. oil to be pumped and sold by seller).

[16] This limit is being raised to $5,000 in some States. Other States still are using the $500 limit.

What is NOT A GOOD? Things that are not moveable (e.g. real estate), fungible items (STOCK, MONEY, NOTES, MORTGAGES, CONTRACTS) and intangible rights (PATENTS, COPYRIGHTS) are not goods. This is true even if the "right" is evidenced by a document that can be moved.

What PERSONAL PROPERTY is NOT A GOOD? Personal property is not a good if it is a "right" like copyrights or timber rights.

Law school professors often have questions that involve two dudes selling a car, a boat or a stereo without intending to create a "UCC" question. But these are GOODS because they are MOVEABLE at the time of identification to the contract, so the UCC applies.

What is NOT covered by Article 2 of the UCC? Contracts for services, stocks, bonds, or real property interests do not involve "goods", and are not governed by Article 2.

What is the application of UCC Article 3? UCC Article 3 (negotiable instruments) is not tested on many State Bar exams, but it does have one important section. Under UCC 3-311 an ACCORD AND SATISFACTION will generally be found, subject to certain exceptions, when there is a good faith dispute over a contract and one party tenders and the other accepts a payment designated to be "payment in full."

> **For example:** Bevis says Butthead owes him $100 and Butthead insists he only owes Bevis $50. Butthead sends Bevis a personal check for $50 that says "payment in full". Bevis cashes the check and writes on it "I object and insist you still owe me $50". Bevis is generally going to be bound to an accord and satisfaction and has no right to pursue his claim further. Understand this principal, and you may need to cite 3-311 on your exam.

What should you do on a contract exam? Unless the call is clear, define "goods", determine whether the item is a good, and say whether UCC Article 2 applies. If there are two companies named Buyco and Sellco, it suggests a sale of goods and they are usually, but not always, merchants. Be sure to explain why to the grader.

The Introductory Contract Statement. Contract essays often ask you to discuss the "rights and remedies" of the parties. This produces awkwardness on how to start. In these "right and remedy" situations start your answer with the following opening statement, <u>VERBATIM</u>:

> *"The rights and remedies of the parties here depend on whether or not they had a valid contract. A CONTRACT is a promise or set of promises, the performance of which the law recognizes as a duty and for the breach of which the law will provide a remedy."*
> **[important!]**

Skip or abbreviate this introductory contract statement to match the call of the question.

COMMON CONTRACT AND UCC ISSUES AND ANSWERS

FOLLOW THE CALL of the question. But if the call is general, such as "discuss the rights and remedies," list the issues as follows:

1. *Does UCC apply?* (**Important!** Always issue #1 if UCC applies, but maybe a "non-issue" otherwise!)

    Under contract law UCC Article 2 controls contracts for the sale of GOODS. Goods are movable things at the time of identification to the contract.[17] *Otherwise only the common law controls.*

    Here the agreement was NOT (is) for a sale of goods, because ….

    Therefore, only the common law (UCC) determines the rights of the parties here.

2. *Are the parties MERCHANTS?* (**Important!** Always issue #2 if UCC applies, but otherwise it is never an issue).

    Under the UCC a MERCHANT is a person who trades in or otherwise holds himself out by occupation or otherwise as knowledgeable about the goods of the contract. Further, a principal that employs an agent that is a merchant is held to be a merchant by implication.[18]

    Here the buyer is (not) a dealer in these goods because … And they are not a merchant by occupation or implication because…Further the seller is (not) a dealer in these goods because… And…Therefore …

3. *Was the communication of* [date] *an OFFER?* (only for a formation question. Watch out for advertisements because they are rarely offers and catalogues are NEVER offers! Skip this altogether if the question says they had an agreement or contract.)

    Under contract law an OFFER is a manifestation of present contractual intent communicated to the offeree such that an objective person would reasonably believe assent would form a bargain. [19] Important!

    If ONLY common law go on to say,

    At common law a communication was only deemed sufficient to constitute an offer if it specified the parties, subject matter, quantity, price, and time of performance.

---

[17] Be aware, and prepared to say, that special made goods, standing crops, timber, unborn animals and minerals in the land to be removed by the seller are also "goods".

[18] For a person in "business" to be a "merchant" they either have to DEAL in the goods that are the subject of the contract on a regular basis or else they have to be some type of "expert" concerning these goods or employ an "agent" who is an expert in these goods.

[19] The reason a "catalogue" is NEVER an offer is that a catalogue is, by definition, a price list without any specification of quantity.

If UCC say,

The UCC deems a communication sufficient to constitute an offer if it specifies the parties and quantity. The UCC provides "GAP FILLERS" that may be used by the Court to determine any additional terms.

Here the communication was (not) an offer because ...

Therefore, the communication was (not) an offer. [20]

4. *Was the offer a MERCHANT'S FIRM OFFER?* (SKIP UNLESS the given facts suggest the offeree may be a merchant and has promised to "leave the offer open" for some period of time)

   Under UCC 2-205 an offer by a merchant that promises to "leave the offer open" for a period of time cannot be revoked by the offeror if it is stated in writing, for the period of time stated, or for a reasonable period of time (given the circumstances) if no time period is stated. However, regardless of the period of time stated by the offeror, the offeror can revoke within 3 months if that is less than the time period stated.

   If the merchant promises to "leave the offer open" for any period of time, whether more or less than 3 months, that is the "reasonable period of time" in which the offeree can accept the offer even if the offeror could legally revoke the offer sooner.

   Here the offer was (not) a merchant's firm offer because...

   Therefore this offer could (not) be revoked on ...

5. *Was it an offer for a UNILATERAL CONTRACT?* (SKIP UNLESS the given facts make it entirely clear this is an intended issue or the offer is a GENERAL OFFER.)

   Under the common law a UNILATERAL CONTRACT OFFER is one that unequivocally indicates acceptance can only be manifested by completion of performance by the offeree. GENERAL OFFERS, reward or bounty offers, are always unilateral contract offers. [21]

   Here it is (not) unequivocally clear that the offeree can only accept this offer by completion of performance because....

   Therefore this is (not) a unilateral contract offer.

6. *Was the communication (action) of [date] an (implied) ACCEPTANCE?* (SKIP if question says there was an agreement or contract.)

   If ONLY common law, say,

   Under the common law MIRROR IMAGE RULE an acceptance is an unequivocal assent to an offer. (However, acceptance can be implied by silent performance.) **Important!**

---

[20] Many law professors use the term "invitation to negotiate" but that has no specific legal meaning. It just means the communication was not legally sufficient to constitute an offer, so that is what you should say.

[21] Do not presume an offer proposes a unilateral contract unless it is a GENERAL OFFER. Otherwise, the offer must be unequivocally clear and if it is not all modern Courts will presume it is a bilateral contract.

If UCC say,

> *Under UCC 2-206 an acceptance of an offer not otherwise expressly conditioned may be made in any REASONABLE MANNER, including a promise to ship or shipment of either conforming or non-conforming goods. BUT a shipment of NON-CONFORMING goods as an EXPRESS ACCOMMODATION is not an acceptance. Further, UCC 2-207 allows an acceptance containing varying terms to be effective.*[22] **Important!**

Here the communication was (not) an acceptance because ...

Therefore, a CONTRACT WAS FORMED on [date]. (Or else the communication was a REJECTION AND COUNTER-OFFER on different terms.)

> **[Note: In a formation question if a contract is formed, it can ONLY be determined by the analysis of the acceptance – that is the only thing that can form a contract.]**

7. *Did the VARYING TERMS become part of the contract?* (Only do this if there is a UCC question and the offeree cites a varying term.)

   Under UCC 2-207 varying terms will NOT be included in the contract where the parties are not both merchants. And even if they are both merchants the varying term still does not become part of the contract if the offer expressly limited acceptance and the offeror does not agree to the new term, OR if the varying terms materially alter the contract, OR if the party to be bound objects to the varying terms within a reasonable period of time.

   If the acceptance is expressly conditioned on the varying terms by the offeree, the response is effectively a rejection and counter-offer. Otherwise the varying terms are considered only "proposed modifications".

   Here the parties are (not) both merchants because... And the acceptance cited varying terms because... Further, the varying terms did (not) materially alter the contract because ...

   Therefore...

8. *Had the OFFER LAPSED before acceptance was attempted?* (This issue is frequently tested and poorly taught.)

   Under common law an offer LAPSES AND CANNOT BE ACCEPTED unless it is accepted in a reasonable period of time. Oral offers are deemed to lapse at the end of the conversation, and written offers are deemed to lapse within the timeframe implied by the means of dispatch, absent contrary agreement or implication.

   Here the offer was oral (by fax, telegraph, mail, etc.) so it would be deemed to have lapsed when ... Therefore the offer did (not) lapse before the offeree attempted to accept it.

---

[22] Pay attention to the difference between "I will" and "I can". In a UCC situation there is an ACCCEPTANCE if the seller says "it will" or "it would" supply the goods, and a REJECTION AND COUNTER-OFFER if the seller says "it can, but..." or "it could, but..." citing a varying term.

9. *Was the communication of [date] an EFFECTIVE ACCEPTANCE?* (SKIP if question says there was an agreement or contract. This is only a possible issue if there is an "acceptance" by "dispatch" that conflicts with some communication of rejection or revocation.)

Under the MAILBOX RULES of the common law an acceptance is effective when dispatched, if dispatched in the manner specified in the offer, or by the same or faster means the offer was transmitted where the offer does not specify a means of communication.

Here the acceptance was (not) effective upon dispatch (receipt) because it was (not) sent by the means specified in the offer (no means was specified in the offer and it was sent at the same or faster means than the offer had been sent).

[Note: a unilateral contract offer can only be accepted by the requested performance, but NEVER assume the offer is for a unilateral contract offer unless it is unequivocal. Further, modern contract law provides SAVING DOCTRINES as stated below.]

Therefore …

10. *Was the communication of* [date] *an EFFECTIVE REJECTION?* (SKIP if not applicable.)

Under the MAILBOX RULES of contract law a rejection is effective upon receipt while an acceptance may be effective upon dispatch. An EXCEPTION is made if the OFFEROR CHANGES POSITION in reliance upon a communication of rejection, not knowing that an acceptance was dispatched prior to receipt of the rejection. In that case the rejection is effective upon receipt regardless of the fact an acceptance was also dispatched.

Here the rejection was (not) effective because …

Here the offeror (did not) change position in reliance on the rejection because…

Therefore …

11. *Was the communication of* [date] *an EFFECTIVE REVOCATION?* (SKIP if not applicable.)

Under the MAILBOX RULES revocation of a contract offer is usually effective upon receipt by the offeree.

For an unequivocal unilateral offer also say, as appropriate,

Under common law a unilateral offer could be revoked at any time, and revocation of GENERAL OFFERS, reward or bounty offers, was effective when published in the same manner the offer was first announced. But modernly SAVING DOCTRINES prevent the revocation of a unilateral contract offer if the offeror is aware the offeree has commenced the requested act for a reasonable period during which the offeree will be allowed to complete acceptance by performance.

Here the offeror was aware the offeree had commenced the requested act because…

Here the revocation was (was not) effective because…Therefore …

12. *Was there an IMPLIED-IN-FACT CONTRACT?*

Under contract law an IMPLIED-IN-FACT CONTRACT will be deemed to have existed, even if there is no express agreement between the parties, if one party acts to bestow benefits on the other party reasonably expecting to be compensated, and the other party knowingly accepts those benefits knowing that the other party expects to be compensated.

An implied-in-fact contract is an actual, legal contract. The party that knowingly receives the benefits is liable for a reasonable contract amount to the other party.

Here…because…Therefore…

13. *Is a WRITING needed?*

If ONLY common law governs say, [23]

Under the STATUTE OF FRAUDS certain types of contracts must be written in order to be legally enforced, and one type is a contract for (pick one if it applies here -- MARRIAGE, more than a YEAR, LAND, EXECUTOR of an estate, GUARANTEE of a debt). [24] **Important!**

If UCC say,

Under UCC 2-201, a contract for sale of goods worth $500 or more must evidenced by a writing sufficient to show the existence of a contract and signed by the party against whom the contract is to be enforced. But between merchants a SALES CONFIRMATION by one listing quantity will bind both parties if the receiving party does not object within 10 days. [25] **Important!**

Furthermore, the UCC provides exceptions for SPECIAL MADE GOODS, where there is an ADMISSION by the party to be bound that there had been an agreement, or where there has been PARTIAL PERFORMANCE of the contract (i.e. acceptance of some or all goods or payment).

Under UCC 2-209 contract modifications must be written to be legally enforceable if the contract, as modified, is for over $500. Otherwise modification agreements will be treated as waivers of conditions that can be always be retracted, unless the Court estops retraction to prevent injustice.

Here the contract is within (is outside) the statute because …

And the need for a writing was (not) satisfied because…

---

[23] The reason I am saying "ONLY common law" is that even UCC contracts are subject to the common law in some manner, but contracts the UCC does NOT apply to will ONLY be controlled by common law.

[24] The mnemonic is MYLEG. The YEAR means from the date of execution until the earliest date the contract could possibly be completed according to its terms. The main issue when there is a GUARANTOR is the "main purpose rule". The main issue when LAND is concerned is whether the "seller" owns any interest in the land that is being conveyed to the "buyer". Note that modernly the a lease of real property for a year or less requires no writing.

[25] Note that the UCC is being modified and in some States this limit is $5,000 while in others it has still been kept at $500.

Therefore, there was (not) a need for a writing in order for the agreement to be legally enforced as a contract, and the requirement was (not) met because... [26]

[Note: The Statute of Frauds is not an "issue" at all when contracts are written. If contracts are oral, addressing the need for a writing early eliminates the danger of forgetting it later. Some professors demand discussion of the need for a writing toward the end of an answer in a "Defenses" section. But when oral contracts cannot be enforced at LAW the movants are forced to plead EQUITY and that will determine your entire essay structure.

If the Statute of Frauds is an issue, the Parol Evidence Rule cannot be an issue, and vice versa since the first is an issue when contracts are oral and the latter when they are written.]

14. *What were the CONTRACT TERMS?*

If an acceptance forms a contract, for common law say,

Under common law enforceable contracts generally must indicate PARTIES, PRICE, SUBJECT MATTER, TIME OF PERFORMANCE and QUANTITY. Most express terms and promises are considered to be EXPRESS MATERIAL CONDITIONS, except for TIME of performance, buyer SATISFACTION, and promises NOT TO ASSIGN the contract which are generally considered mere "covenants".

If an acceptance forms a contract, for UCC say,

Under the UCC a contract is enforceable if the QUANTITY and PARTIES are specified. Other terms will be provided by the GAP FILLER provisions of the UCC. All express terms and promises are treated as material terms under the PERFECT TENDER RULE.

Here the PARTIES to the contract were..., the QUANTITY was..., the PRICE was ..., SUBJECT MATTER was.. , and TIME OF PERFORMANCE was ...

Therefore, the contract was (not) specified enough to be enforceable.

15. *Was TIMELY PERFORMANCE a MATERIAL CONDITION?* (This is frequently tested and poorly taught. This is never a UCC issue because under the Perfect Tender Rule tardy performance is always a breach.)

Under contract law the parties may agree at the time of contract execution that timely performance (by the party to first perform contract services) is a MATERIAL CONDITION. Then the condition is called an EXPRESS CONDITION, and typically the contract says, "Time is of the essence".

But material conditions may also be or implied when the parties knew at the time of execution that tardy performance would deny the non-performing party the BENEFIT OF THE

---

[26] While "defenses" are often saved for the end of the essay, this one is so important it is best to address it early in the essay when you have plenty of time. If you wait to the end of the essay before you address this issue and run out of time it may be fatal to your law school career.

BARGAIN, the benefit expected when they entered into the agreement. In that case the condition is called an IMPLIED MATERIAL CONDITION.

Here the parties did (not) agree that "time was of the essence". And tardy performance would (not) deny the non-breaching party the benefit of the bargain because...

Therefore...

> **[Note: The INTENT of the parties at the time of execution is the court's only concern, NOT the actual EFFECT of tardy execution. If the contract concerns the performance of services that are frequently delayed by weather, transportation delays or other factors beyond the control of the parties the Court will generally assume timely performance was NOT a material condition unless the terms of the contract expressly say it is.]**

16. Was Buyer SATISFACTION a MATERIAL CONDITION? (This is frequently tested and poorly taught.)

Under contract law reasonably satisfactory performance by the parties is ALWAYS AN IMPLIED MATERIAL CONDITON of every contract. However, the parties may agree that buyer SATISFACTION is a MATERIAL CONDITION so buyers who are not actually satisfied have no legal duty to pay.

But if the terms of the agreement do not expressly and unequivocally state that the parties intended for personal satisfaction to be a material condition, the Court will generally hold that a promise of "satisfaction" was merely a "covenant" to perform in a manner that would be satisfactory to a "reasonable person" and NOT a material condition UNLESS the service to be performed was one that is highly subject to personal tastes.

Here the parties did (not) expressly agree that "satisfaction" was a material condition. And the service to be performed was not one that is highly subject to personal tastes. **[Or else, *"But the service to be performed was one that is highly subject to personal tastes."*]**

Therefore...

> **[Note: The types of services that are highly subject to personal tastes are things such as portrait photographs and artistic renderings. Otherwise, a Court is generally going to interpret a promise of "satisfaction" to mean a promise (covenant) to perform in a manner satisfactory to a reasonable person, absent express, unequivocal language to the contrary in the contract.]**

17. Does the PAROL EVIDENCE RULE bar evidence of other covenants and terms? (This is only an issue if there is a detailed written contract. This and the Statute of Frauds can almost never both be issues in the same fact pattern because usually the contract can only be either written or oral, not both at the same time.)

Under the PAROL EVIDENCE RULE evidence of PRIOR or CONTEMPORANEOUS agreements may not be introduced to VARY or CONTRADICT the terms of a FULLY INTEGRATED WRITING unless it is to show evidence of **[DAM FOIL]** *Duress, Ambiguity,*

Mistake, Fraud, Oral condition precedent, Illegality, or Lack of consideration.[27] *The Court may determine the "completeness" of a written contract by examining the comprehensiveness of its contents.*

Here ...because...Therefore...

18. *Can LACK OF INTENT be raised as a defense?*

Under the OBJECTIVE MAN RULE, there is sufficient INTENT to enter into a contract if an objective observer listening to the parties would have reasonably concluded from their communications that assent would form a bargain.

Here an objective observer would (not) have thought the party to be bound intended to form a contract because...Therefore...

19. *Is LACK OF CONSIDERATION a defense?* (This is almost never a worthwhile issue in a UCC answer except for a modification scenario because the original contract always involves an exchange of goods for money so how can there be a lack of consideration at that point?)

Under contract law every valid contract, and any modification of a contract, must be supported by CONSIDERATION, a BARGAINED FOR exchange posing sufficient LEGAL DETRIMENT that the law will enforce the agreement.[28] **Important!**

For UCC modification say,

> *However, under the UCC a contract supported by legal consideration may be MODIFIED without additional consideration."*

Here the promised act was (not) bargained for because...

And there was (not) any legal detriment to the promisee because he had (did not have) a PRE-EXISTING DUTY to...

Further [party] was (not) totally denied the benefit of the bargain because...

Therefore, the contract did (not) fail for lack of consideration.

---

[27] 90% of law students have no idea what an "oral condition precedent" is, and it is the most tested of all of these possibilities. It is an oral agreement that a contract party does not have to perform a stated contractual duty UNLESS the condition holds. It is like an oral agreement that you don't have to pay your student loans if you don't pass the Bar Exam.

[28] Consideration is an "exchange" or "quid pro quo" so any promise of a gift, or even an exchange between parties of promises to bestow gifts on each other, is not valid, legal consideration. The vast majority of Courts hold that "past acts" and "moral obligation" are NOT valid consideration. A promise exchanged for a promise is always considered adequate consideration, as long as each promise is not merely to do something that the other party already had a legal duty to perform. But if a party's promise is "illusory" or "empty" the contract is void from the beginning for "lack of consideration". And otherwise if a party fails to perform the promised duty so completely that the other party gets no benefit at all, that is a major breach and again the contract may be said to have failed for "lack of consideration".

[Note: This is never a UCC issue as to the original contract because it is always a trade of money for goods (that is what makes it a UCC situation). So it can only be an issue in a "UCC question" when there is a modification of the original contract, and then no consideration is required so it is a marginal issue then, also.]

20. *Was the need for a WRITING SATISFIED?* (This second visit to the Statute of Frauds is only necessary if you did not settle the issue completely at the beginning of the essay OR there has been a contract modification.)

    As discussed above, this contract would have to be supported by a signed writing under the STATUTE OF FRAUDS (or UCC 2-201) sufficient to show the existence and required terms of the contract.

    For UCC modification say,

    > *Under UCC 2-209 contract modifications do not require consideration, but if a contract as modified would have to be supported by a sufficient writing under UCC 2-201, and the modification is not supported by a writing, it is not enforceable at law. However, the modification may be viewed by the Court as a WAIVER OF CONDITION that the waiving party has a legal right to retract, but the Court may estop the retraction of the waiver of condition to prevent injustice.*

    Here there was (not) a sufficient writing to enforce the contract (or modification) because... Therefore ...

21. *Was the contract UNCONSCIONABLE?* (Never discuss this unless the given facts make it very, very clear it is an intended issue.)

    Under contract law an unconscionable contract will not be enforceable because there is NO REASONABLE FINDING OF INTENT to enter into such a contract. An ADHESION CONTRACT is a "take it or leave it" contract that a party is forced to agree to, and it will often be found unenforceable.

    Here the contract appears to be unconscionable because ...Therefore ...

22. *Is DURESS a defense?*

    Under contract law only good faith agreements are enforceable. No contract agreement induced by illegal threats is valid. Likewise, agreements induced by deliberate acts to create threats of economic harm are not enforceable.[29]

    Here the contract may be argued to be unconscionable (or the result of duress) because...

    Therefore ...

---

[29] You are unlikely to ever see a question that suggests threats of physical harm because the answer is too easy. But remember that a contract creates legal duties to perform so a threat to breach a contract is an illegal threat. Any agreement that results is the result of "economic duress" and is unenforceable.

23. *Is FRAUD (or DECEIT) a defense?*

Under contract law a contract induced through deliberate CONCEALMENT of material facts by a party with a duty to reveal the facts, or by a party deliberately concealing and/or MISREPRESENTING material facts is unenforceable if it can be shown the party seeking to void the contract would never have agreed to the bargain but for the concealment and/or misrepresentation. [30]

Here there was (not) fraud because ...Therefore ...

24. *Is INCAPACITY a defense?*

Under contract law a contract cannot be enforced AGAINST one who lacks capacity. EXCEPTIONS are contracts for provision of NECESSITIES of life and where the incapacitated party attains capacity (becomes sane or an adult) and either AFFIRMS or FAILS TO REPUDIATE the contract. [31]

Here the party seeking to avoid the contract was a MINOR (or ADJUDICATED INSANE perhaps) at the time the contract was executed because... And (But) the contract was not (was) for necessities of life because... [32] *And (But) the party to be bound did (not) ratify the contract because...* [33]

Therefore, this contract could (not) be enforced.

25. *Is ILLEGALITY a defense?*

Under contract law, a contract generally cannot be enforced by a party who knowingly entered into it for an illegal purpose. If the parties are equally guilty, IN PARI DELICTO, the court will generally not intervene. However, if one party is less guilty, the court has discretion to order restitution in equity.

Here ... because ...Therefore ...

26. *Is IMPOSSIBILITY a defense?*

Under contract law a material condition of every contract is that performance of contract duties must be objectively possible to perform. The inability of a contract party to perform is irrelevant, as long as performance, in general, is possible. But if performance becomes impossible because of events beyond the control of the parties the contract becomes void. [34]
Here ... because ...Therefore ...

---

[30] Fraud based on misrepresentation is easy to claim but hard to prove because the movant has the burden of proving the other party intended to defraud them at the time of contract. But fraud based on concealment is much easier to prove because the movant usually only has to prove that the other party knew the facts, had a duty to reveal the facts, and did not reveal the facts.

[31] Note that a contract with an incapacitated party is VALID but possibly unenforceable against that party.

[32] Necessities of life means food, shelter, clothing, medical care, etc. NOT legal representation.

[33] If a previously incapacitated party continues to enjoy the benefits of a contract after the incapacity is removed they may be deemed to have "impliedly ratified" the contract.

[34] A MATERIAL CONDITION of every contract is that performance is not required if it is impossible. Impossibility does not have to be "unforeseeable". It just has to result from events beyond the parties' control.

27. *Is COMMERCIAL IMPRACTICABILITY a defense?*

A Court (a judge, in equity) has the authority to declare a contract void if performance by a party would be so financially burdensome, because of events beyond the control of the parties, that it would cause an injustice. Here…because…Therefore…

28. *Is FRUSTRATION OF PURPOSE a defense?*

Under contract law, if the parties enter into a contract knowing that the failure of some condition beyond their control will deny one of the parties the benefit of the bargain, that condition is an implied material condition of the contract, the failure of which excuses both parties from the agreement .[35] Here … because …Therefore …

29. *Is MUTUAL MISTAKE a defense?*

Under PEERLESS when both parties enter into a contract because of a misunderstanding as to a material fact, there is no "meeting of the minds" and the contract is void from the beginning.[36] Here … because … Therefore …

30. *Is UNILATERAL MISTAKE a defense?*

Under contract law, when one party enters into a contract because of a misunderstanding as to a material fact the majority view is that the parties are legally bound to the contract unless the other party knew or should have known of the mistake, and in that case the contract is voidable by the mistaken party. Under a minority view the contract is legally voidable by the mistaken party in any event if they 1) discover the mistake quickly before the other party substantially relies on the contract, 2) give prompt notice of the mistake, and 3) reimburse the other party for any expenses caused by the mistake.[37] Here…because…Therefore….

31. *Was there an ANTICIPATORY BREACH?* (If there is also a WAIVER of the breach, discuss both issues together.)

Under contract law an anticipatory breach (or anticipatory repudiation) is a CLEAR STATEMENT OR INDICATION that a party WILL NOT PERFORM future contractual duties when they become due. This is a major breach as to those duties, the non-breaching party is EXCUSED from performance of all remaining contractual duties, and the future duties of the breaching party are ACCELERATED to the present.

---

[35] This is a second example of failure of an IMPLIED MATERIAL CONDITION. The famous case was the renting of an apartment to see the procession of the newly crowned king. When the king became ill the rental contract was without purpose. Lack of foreseeability was not necessary. All that is needed is that both parties know the purpose of the party seeking to void the contract, and that that party had no control over the failure of the condition.

[36] A mutual mistake means that BOTH parties shared a misunderstanding of facts that were material to the purpose and effect of the contract, and in that case the contract is void from the beginning. For example, if A agrees to sell a painting to B, and both think the painting is by Picasso, then the contract will be void from the beginning if the painting is not by Picasso.

[37] Under the majority view a mistaken party that breaches will be legally liable for "expectation" and "reliance" damages of the other party unless they can obtain equitable relief. But under the minority view (based on the California case of *Elsinore v. Kastorff*) the mistaken party can legally rescind and is only liable for the "reliance" damages.

If a party has a REASONABLE BASIS to believe the other party may not perform future contractual duties, the party may demand REASONABLE ASSURANCES and REFUSE TO PERFORM until they are provided. Reasonable assurances generally means a financial guarantee or payment into escrow.

If reasonable assurances are properly demanded and not provided, the failure to respond constitutes an anticipatory breach.

Here there was (not) an anticipatory breach because the party said "...." and that (did not) make it clear they were not going to perform. That did (not) form a reasonable basis for (the other party) to demand reasonable assurances because... Therefore...

32. *WAIVER of the breach?* (Discuss if anticipatory breach is ignored by non-breaching party.)

Under contract law if a non-breaching party lets the breaching party continue performance after a major breach it WAIVES THE BREACH.[38] *The waiver cannot be revoked, and the non-breaching party is forever ESTOPPED from citing the breach as major and can only cite it as a minor breach. Here ... because ...Therefore...*

33. *Was there a BREACH OF IMPLIED COVENANT?*

An IMPLIED MATERIAL CONDITION of every contract is that the parties must act in good faith and are bound by an IMPLIED COVENANT that they will act as reasonably necessary to help the other parties enjoy the benefits of the contract and that they will not act in any way to prevent that from occurring.

A breach of GOOD FAITH or acting in "bad faith" means either deceit, concealment or fraud at the time of execution or else the breach of an implied covenant. The mere breach of an express contract promise, even if done deliberately, is not a breach of good faith.

Here ... Therefore...

34. *BREACH? MAJOR OR MINOR?* (Realize the first party to breach a contract is the breaching party and after that the other party is the non-breaching party no matter what they do later.)

For COMMON LAW say,

Under contract law a BREACH is a failure to perform a contractual duty when it becomes due. A MAJOR BREACH is either an act which deprives the other party of the BENEFIT OF THE BARGAIN or the violation of an EXPRESS OR IMPLIED MATERIAL CONDITION by a party, regardless of its effect on the other party. A major breach EXCUSES the non-breaching party from all further performance of contractual duties and ACCELERATES the future contractual duties of the breaching party to the present so the non-breaching party can seek IMMEDIATE PAYMENT OF DAMAGES.

[38] Technically this is an "election" and not a "waiver" but everyone calls it a "waiver of breach".

For UCC say,

Under the PERFECT TENDER RULE of the UCC any shipment of non-conforming goods is a breach of contract. There is no distinction between "major" and "minor" breaches.

For UCC DIVISIBLE CONTRACT SITUATION say,

Under the UCC a breach with respect to any shipment of goods under a DIVISIBLE CONTRACT does not constitute a breach of the entire contract. A DIVISIBLE contract is one under which goods are to be delivered in separate shipments which can each be evaluated separately under the contract.

Here ... because ...Therefore...

35. <u>EFFECT OF BREACH ON A DIVISIBLE CONTRACT?</u>

Under the UCC a breach with respect to any shipment of goods under a DIVISIBLE CONTRACT does not constitute a breach of the entire contract. A DIVISIBLE contract is one under which goods are to be delivered in separate shipments which can each be evaluated separately under the contract.

Here there was a divisible UCC contract because...Therefore...

36. <u>WAIVER of condition</u>?

Under contract law if a party performs a contractual duty that is subject to a condition precedent at a time the condition fails to hold, the party WAIVES THE CONDITION. But after a condition has been waived the waiving party has a legal right to retract the waiver. [39] *Nevertheless, a Court of EQUITY may estop the retraction based on considerations of equitable estoppel.* (UCC 2-209 adopts this same concept when oral contract modifications fail to meet the requirements of UCC 2-201. See "Is a Writing Needed?" above.)

Here ... because ...Therefore.

37. <u>Was there an ACCORD AND SATISFACTION?</u>

Under contract law an ACCORD AND SATISFACTION is binding on both parties if there is an <u>agreement</u> by the parties to settle a <u>reasonable</u> and <u>good faith</u> claim by one party that the other party has breached the original contract. [40]

Here a claim of breach was raised in <u>good faith</u> because ... And it was <u>reasonable</u> because... And there was an <u>agreement</u> in settlement because...Therefore...

---

[39] For example, Bevis and Butthead have a labor contract that says Bevis will pay Butthead's wages on Fridays. Bevis' does not have any duty to pay Butthead unless it is Friday. But one week Bevis pays Butthead on Thursday. That "waives the condition" for that week. But Bevis does not have to pay Butthead every Thursday after that because he can "retract the waiver".

[40] Further, under UCC 3-311 acceptance or cashing a "check" marked "satisfaction in full" or something similar generally discharges all liability. There are exceptions, but this UCC provision reflects the common law view.

38. Is the plaintiff an INTENDED THIRD-PARTY BENEFICIARY?

Under contract law an INTENDED THIRD-PARTY BENEFICIARY is a party that can seek damages for breach of a contract between two other parties because the contract was INTENDED to benefit them.

An INCIDENTAL beneficiary, one that was not intended to benefit from a contract between others, has no ability to enforce the contract or seek damages.

Contracts can only be enforced by VESTED, INTENDED third-party beneficiaries that are DONEES, intended to benefit as a GIFT, or CREDITORS, intended to benefit by EXTINGUISHING A DEBT.

At common law vesting was a more demanding requirement than it is modernly. Under the modern view VESTING occurs if the beneficiary becomes aware of and relies on the existence of the contract.

Here ___ was (not) an intended third-party beneficiary because... And he (did not) become vested because...

Therefore ...

39. STANDING based on a VALID ASSIGNMENT? [41]

Under contract law an ASSIGNEE can seek damages for breach of a contract from the contract promisor if the assignee was EXPRESSLY ASSIGNED the rights of an original promisee, the ASSIGNOR, by EXPRESSION OF CLEAR INTENT.

An assignment BECOMES EFFECTIVE when the assignee gives the promisor NOTICE of the specific rights assigned. When the assignment becomes effective the promisor is liable only to the assignee and the rights of the original promisee/assignor are EXTINGUISHED.

If the assignment was in exchange for CONSIDERATION given by the assignee to the promisee/assignor, the assignment is IRREVOCABLE, and it creates a legal contract between the assignee and the promisee/assignor. That contract creates implied warranties 1) that the rights assigned exist, 2) that the promisee/assignor has the authority to assign them, and 3) all documents provided are bone fide. The assignee may seek legal damages from the assignor for a breach of warranty.

If the assignment was GRATUITOUS it is REVOCABLE until the assignment is made 1) in writing, 2) a token chose is delivered, or 3) detrimental reliance makes revocation inequitable. A gratuitous assignment creates no implied warranties and can only be enforced in equity.

Here ... because ...Therefore ...

[41] If a question says a party that has a current duty to perform (e.g. to build a house) "assigned the contract" to another party that is going to perform the promised duties, then both an ASSIGMENT of rights and a DELEGATION of duties are implied. These should be discussed as two separate issues.

[Note: Assignment, delegation and other third-party questions require that you identify the parties and explain all of the rights and liabilities each party has against the other parties. That usually takes so much time that there is little time left for anything else.]

40. *VALID DELEGATION of performance?*

Under contract law the duty to perform under a contract may be DELEGATED to a DELEGATEE by an original promisor/delegator. However, the promisor/delegator remains primarily liable to the original promisee for performance of the contract. The delegation becomes EFFECTIVE when the delegatee agrees to perform the duties of the promisor/delegator.

If the delegatee accepts the delegation in exchange for CONSIDERATION, a legal contract is created between the promisor/delegator and the delegatee, and the original promisee is an intended third-party beneficiary of that contract. As an intended third-party beneficiary the promisee has standing to pursue legal actions against both the promisor/delegator and the delegatee.

If the delegatee GRATUITOUSLY accepts the delegation the delegatee has no legal liability to the original promisee and the promisee can only enforce the delegation agreement in equity by showing detrimental reliance.

Here ... because ...Therefore ...

41. *Effect of ASSIGNMENT on CLAIMS AND DEFENSES?*

Under contract law a promisor may generally assert any claim or defense against the assignee that could have been asserted against the promisee/assignor. [42]

Here...because...Therefore...

42. *Effect of MODIFICATION AFTER ASSIGNMENT?*

MODIFICATION of a contract after it has been assigned is generally effective against the assignee if 1) the contract has not yet been fully performed, and 2) the modification is made in good faith and in accordance with reasonable commercial standards. The assignee acquires CORRESPONDING RIGHTS under the modified (or substituted) contract. [43]

---

[42] The provisions of UCC Article 9 expressly control this and establish various exceptions. But that Article is NOT TESTED on all Bar exams. So the rule statement above should be sufficient unless your State tests on Article 9.

[43] This is also a UCC Article 9 issue that is note expressly tested on all State Bar exams, but the issue could still arise.

43. *COMMON LAW REMEDY of the NON-BREACHING PARTY?* [44]

Under common law the non-breaching party has a right to COMPENSATORY DAMAGES calculated as the sum of 1) RELIANCE DAMAGES, out-of-pocket expenses the non-breaching party paid before the breach in reliance on the contract, 2) EXPECTATION DAMAGES, the expected benefits of the contract lost because of the breach, 3) INCIDENTAL DAMAGES, out-of-pocket expenses the non-breaching party paid because of the breach (e.g. storage costs) and 4) CONSEQUENTIAL DAMAGES, lost profits on collateral contracts that failed because of the breach. **[Note: Don't go into all of this in detail about the measure of damages unless the given facts give you the sort of detailed monetary loss information you need.]**

Non-breaching parties must prove their damages with substantial CERTAINTY, that they were CAUSED by the breach, and COULD NOT HAVE BEEN AVOIDED. This is sometimes called the DUTY TO MITIGATE damages.

If the breaching party has SUBSTANTIALLY PERFORMED, the non-breaching party is still obligated under the contract with an OFFSET for damages against the contract price. But if the breaching party is in MAJOR BREACH the non-breaching party is freed from all obligations under the contract and has a right to an award of all damages caused.

A non-breaching buyer of unique property such as land or services can also ask for an order of SPECIFIC PERFORMANCE to obtain title, possession or performance. There is no "right" to specific performance. It is an equitable remedy at the judge's discretion. Specific performance cannot be used to force performance of personal services by an individual because it violates the 13th Amendment, but an organization (e.g. corporation) may be ordered by the Court to perform unique services. ... Here...because...Therefore...

44. *CONSEQUENTIAL DAMAGES?*

Under HADLEY V. BAXENDALE, a party to a contract may recover CONSEQUENTIAL DAMAGES such as LOST PROFITS expected from collateral contracts that fail because the contract was breached only if it can be shown the damages were **[CCCC]** *1) CONTEMPLATED (foreseen) by both parties at the time of contract, 2) CERTAIN (measurable) as to dollar value, 3) CLEARLY CAUSED by (resulting from) the breach and 4) the loss COULDN'T BE AVOIDED. ... Here...because...Therefore...*

45. *COMMON LAW REMEDY of the BREACHING PARTY?*

Under common law a breaching party that has SUBSTANTIALLY PERFORMED has a right to recover the CONTRACT PRICE LESS AN OFFSET for damages caused by the breach. The remedy of a party in MAJOR BREACH is to seek RESTITUTION for AMOUNTS PAID and BENEFITS CONFERRED to the extent they exceed the damages of the non-breaching party, to prevent UNJUST ENRICHMENT. ... Here...because...Therefore...

---

[44] It is usually best to discuss remedies from the aspect of the non-breaching party. Your explanation must be tailored to fit the particular facts. In the usual case there is substantial performance and the non-breaching party only has a right to an offset. If there is a major breach the non-breaching party has no obligation to pay anything except restitution to the extent they have benefited from partial performance.

46. *UCC REMEDY of the NON-BREACHING BUYER?*

Under the PERFECT TENDER RULE of the UCC a non-breaching buyer can either ACCEPT or REJECT non-conforming goods. Also they can REPUDIATE the contract and COVER, or they can AFFIRM the contract and DEMAND CONFORMING GOODS. The measure of damages is the excess, if any, of market or cover price over the contract price. If the goods are unique non-breaching buyers can ask for an order of SPECIFIC PERFORMANCE to obtain title and possession. There is no "right" to specific performance.

Here ... because... Therefore...

47. *UCC REMEDY of the NON-BREACHING SELLER?*

Under the UCC a non-breaching seller can sell rejected but conforming goods at a PUBLIC OR PRIVATE SALVAGE SALE (with NOTICE TO BREACHING BUYER) and demand the excess, if any, of the CONTRACT PRICE over the SALVAGE SALE price.

Alternatively, in a LOST-VOLUME SITUATION where sellers cannot effectively sell the same goods to someone else, they can demand the BENEFIT OF THE BARGAIN of their "lost profits" – the excess, if any, of the CONTRACT PRICE over their cost of acquiring the goods.

And if the goods have been special made or for some other reason can not be sold elsewhere the non-breaching seller can "sue on the contract price" to get a judgment for that amount.

Here ... because ...Therefore...

48. *UCC REMEDY of the BREACHING SELLER?*

Under the UCC a breaching seller that GIVES NOTICE of an intent to cure has an absolute right to cure the breach WITHIN THE CONTRACT PERIOD, and also has a right to REASONABLE EXTRA TIME in which to cure beyond the contract period if non-conforming goods have been shipped with a reasonable belief they would satisfy the needs of the buyer.

Here ... because...Therefore...

49. *Is the LIQUIDATED DAMAGES clause enforceable?*

LIQUIDATED DAMAGES CLAUSES specify that the sole remedy of the non-breaching party is a specified amount of money damages. These clauses are only enforceable if 1) DAMAGES arising from a breach were UNCERTAIN at the TIME OF CONTRACT, 2) the specified amount was REASONABLE at the time of contract, and 3) enforcement after a breach will provide a REASONABLE REMEDY for the non-breaching party.

Liquidated damages clauses in contracts for UNIQUE PROPERTY are generally UNENFORCEABLE because money damages are inadequate and SPECIFIC PERFORMANCE is appropriate.[45] *... Here ... because ...Therefore ...*

[45] This is frequently tested and poorly taught. Liquidated damages will almost NEVER be a reasonable remedy for a non-breaching buyer if the contract is for unique property. But they are often enforceable against breaching buyers.

50. *Was there an IMPLIED-IN-LAW CONTRACT?*

An IMPLIED-IN-LAW CONTRACT is an equitable theory or "cause of action" which gives the Court discretion to provide an equitable remedy when there is no valid, legally enforceable contract if the moving party has acted to convey benefits to the responding party with a reasonable expectation of being compensated in return.

The Court may either award the amount necessary to prevent an unjust enrichment to the respondent, or the amount necessary to prevent frustration of the reasonable expectations of the movant.

Here…because…Therefore…

[Note: This argument should only be raised when no contract is otherwise enforceable at law. Perhaps there was a contract that violated the Statute of Frauds, there was a major breach, or the respondent lacked legal capacity. This equitable theory requires that the movant reasonably expected to be paid for services rendered.]

51. *Can PROMISSORY ESTOPPEL be pled?*

PROMISSORY ESTOPPEL is an equitable theory or "cause of action" which gives the Court discretion to provide an equitable remedy when there is no valid, legally enforceable contract or other legal cause of action but the moving party has acted in reasonable reliance on a promise by the respondent, the respondent intended to induce the movant to rely on the promise, and justice demands that the promise be enforced to some degree.

The Court may either enforce the promise or award the amount necessary to prevent an unjust enrichment to the respondent, or the amount necessary to prevent frustration of the reasonable expectations of the movant.

Here…because…Therefore…

[Note: This argument should only be raised when the movant seeks to enforce an express promise by the respondent and there is no basis for a tort action for fraud or deceit. Often the promise is a gift promise or an assurance the respondent will not assert some legal defense or institute some legal action.]

52. *Can DETRIMENTAL RELIANCE be pled?*

DETRIMENTAL RELIANCE is an equitable theory or "cause of action" which gives the Court discretion to provide an equitable remedy when there is no valid, legally enforceable contract or other legal cause of action, but the moving party has acted in reasonable reliance on EITHER deliberately false representations of fact by the respondent OR deliberately misleading behavior of the respondent done with intent to induce reliance by the movant, and justice demands that the promise be enforced to some degree.

The Court may award the amount necessary to prevent an unjust enrichment to the respondent, or the amount necessary to prevent frustration of the reasonable expectations of the movant.

Here…because…Therefore…

[Note: This argument should only be raised when there is no "promise" at all, and no other basis to claim either implied-in-law contract or promissory estoppel. The key element here is that the respondent must act (or refrain from acting) with deliberate intent to cause the movant to rely on either false statements of fact or else misleading behavior.]

53. *Is EQUITABLE RESTITUTION appropriate?*

EQUITABLE RESTITUTION is a remedy awarded by a Court of EQUITY when the parties have no adequate legal remedy. The purpose may be to compensate for injuries suffered, prevent unjust enrichment, prevent frustration of reasonable expectations, or restore the status quo.

Here … because …Therefore …

[Note: This issue should only be raised when the contract is not otherwise enforceable at law and a money judgment or other remedy is necessary to prevent injustice. Equitable restitution is a remedy (what the Court does), not an "equitable theory" or "cause of action" that justifies the remedy (why the Court does it).]

54. *Is SPECIFIC PERFORMANCE appropriate?*

SPECIFIC PERFORMANCE is an equitable remedy. It is an order of the Court directing parties to deliver possession and title to unique property. A business organization (not an individual) may also be ordered to provide unique services. This may arise out of an action base on a legally enforceable contract or out of an action based on an equitable theory (equitable cause of action). In either case, there is no "right" to specific performance but the Court (judge) has discretion to order it if award of a money judgment would not be an adequate remedy, perhaps because the property (or services) in dispute are unique.

Here … because …Therefore …

Note: The above issue statements provide almost every important issue, definition, rule and term that you will ever see on a CONTRACTS examination in law school or Bar exam. If you know the above issues and responses you have everything you really need. However, for Bar exams you should also briefly review the remaining UCC sections.

Practice Question 16-1

Lucy owned a rent house. She advertised in the newspaper to find a renter, citing rent of $700 a month.

Homer saw the ad and called Lucy at 9:00 a.m. Homer said, “"I saw your ad and accept your offer! I will be right there to pay you. I have to see the house, but would you consider $550?”

Lucy said, “It's a deal. I will rent to you for $550. This is a firm offer.” Homer said he would be there in one hour to see the house.

Homer went 100 miles an hour to see the house, sideswiping Victoria. Victoria crashed and died along with her 7-month fetus.

At 3:00 p.m. Homer arrived, five hours late, ran up to Lucy and said, “I unequivocally accept. Here is my $550.”

Lucy said, “I have decided not to rent to you.”

Discuss the rights of Homer and Lucy's defenses.

Practice Question 16-2

Al had bought a lot of clothes over the years. One day he called tailor Bob and asked him to custom make him a tuxedo to wear to the wedding of his daughter Carla the next Sunday.

Bob told Al that he could not make a tuxedo so fast and suggested instead that Al buy a ready-made tuxedo that he had in stock in exactly Al's size. Al agreed and said he would be in to pick it up later that week. Price was not discussed.

Bob sent Al a note several days later stating, "This is to confirm your order to purchase the tuxedo. The price is normally $750, but for you the price is only $519.95."

Al was shocked at the price, but it was too late for him to get a tuxedo anywhere else on such short notice. He felt he had been taken advantage of, but there was nothing he could do.

Al came in and tried the tuxedo on the day before the wedding and it did not fit. Bob assured him not to worry. He would take it in. Al nodded.

Bob took in the pants and sent Al a note that said, "I took in the pants and it should fit you like a glove. With alterations the price is now $750.

Al was furious.

Carla's wedding was suddenly called off. Al never called Bob and never went to get the tuxedo. Bob was furious.

Does Bob have a right to be paid for the tuxedo? What are Al's defenses?

Practice Question 16-3

Groucho entered into a contract with new car dealer Harpo to buy a new Dodge for his brother Chico on his birthday. The agreed sales price was $25,000. Harpo promised the new car would be delivered by Chico's birthday within two weeks. Chico was ecstatic. Groucho made a down payment of $2,000 and promised to pay an additional amount of $23,000 for the car over a five-year period.

Harpo made a deal with another dealer, Swifty. Swifty agreed to deliver a Dodge of the type specified on time for Chico's birthday in exchange for an immediate payment of $20,000.

Swifty became insolvent, its inventory was seized and it did not deliver the Dodge.

Harpo blames Swifty.

Chico was upset he didn't get the car he expected.

What are the rights, remedies and defenses of Groucho, Harpo, Chico and Swifty?

Practice Question 16-4

When Al was in high school he wrote and copyrighted a rap song called "Dumb and Dead." He submitted his song to talent agent Tom. On January 1, two days before his seventeenth birthday, he and Tom reached a valid oral agreement that Tom could have exclusive recording rights until Al was 18 years old. Tom was to receive 25 percent of "sales."

Tom sent Al a signed, written "sales confirmation" of their agreement that gave all of the details of the agreement. The memo pointed out that records are "goods" under the UCC. After this Al performed completely under the terms of the agreement.

Tom pitched Al's song to Deccra Records telling them Al was 19 years old, an adult. Following negotiations by Tom, Deccra and Al signed a written agreement on March 1 that Al would receive 50 percent of gross record sales over the next three years. Deccra was aware that Tom would receive a portion of this money under his contract with Al.

Before Deccra paid anything it discovered Al was only 17. A Deccra executive secretly met with Al and told him the company would not stand by its first agreement, and an alternative agreement was proposed that would benefit both parties. Al agreed on April 1 to a new arrangement under which he got 40 percent of gross record sales, Deccra got 60 percent and Tom was cut completely out.

The song went straight to the top of the charts and Deccra's sales were $1.6 million in the next year. Of this amount Deccra paid Al $640,000, 40 percent of gross sales. Deccra's distribution expenses were $360,000, and it made profits of $600,000. Tom got nothing.

Tom got a lawyer and sued both Al and Deccra.

Al also went to a lawyer. Six months after becoming an adult on his eighteenth birthday he sued Deccra claiming he was a minor when the contract was signed. He demanded return of all remaining revenues, $960,000.

1) Was the contract of January 1 unenforceable by Tom because it was oral?
2) Was the contract of January 1 enforceable against Tom by Al?
3) Was the contract of March 1 enforceable by Al against Deccra?
4) Was the contract of April 1 enforceable by Deccra against Al?
5) If the contract of April 1 is legally unenforceable by Deccra, what equitable argument might it make?

Practice Question 16-5

Homeowner Homer orally agreed with builder Bill that he would pay Bill $100,000 to have a custom built home erected on the land that Homer already owned. They agreed the home was to be done before the winter rains set in.

When Bill was half done building, he discovered he had terminal cancer and would only live a few weeks.

Bill told Homer his medical expenses were so high he needed $30,000 more in order to hire a helper or it would be impossible for him to finish the home in time. Homer offered to pay Bill the extra $30,000 this would take because he was tired of living in a tent.

In reasonable reliance on Homer's promise, Bill hired his friend, Fred, and paid Fred wages of $30,000.

The home was all done except for the painting when Bill died. Fred split.

Homer demanded that Bill's widow, Wanda, as executor of Bill's estate, finish the house. She said it was impossible.

Wanda demanded payment of $130,000, but Homer was mad and refused to pay anything.

Homer paid painter Paul $10,000 to finish the painting of the home.

Discuss the rights and defenses of Homer and Wanda against each other.

Practice Question 16-6

Dottie's father Fester called her one day and told her he had suffered a stroke. He was paralyzed from the scalp down. He asked her to come live with him and take care of him. He told her that if, and only if, she took care of him for the rest of his life he would leave her his entire estate in his will, including his house. He emphasized that Dottie could only accept his offer by doing what he asked, and that she could not accept by merely promising to take care of him.

Dottie sold her home at a $50,000 loss and moved across the country to take care of Fester for the rest of his life. She gave up her $250,000 per year practice as a brain surgeon nursed Fester 24 hours a day, seven days a week. Similar care in a nursing home would have cost $40,000 per year.

After ten years Fester suddenly said, "I revoke! Get out of my house." Dottie sadly moved into a homeless shelter.

A month later Fester died leaving his estate, consisting of the house and 1 million shares of Microsoft, to TV evangelist, Reverend Melvin Huckster, and his Society for the Prevention of Cat Teasing.

Discuss
1) Dottie's remedies at law relative to the stock?
2) Dottie's remedies at law relative to the house?
3) Her remedies for enforcement at equity?
4) Her remedies in alternative to enforcement?

Practice Question 16-7

Sellco sent Buyco a catalogue offering widgets at $6 with a 90-day warranty.

On 6/2/99 Buyco wrote Sellco and said, "We hereby accept your catalogue offer and order 10,000 yellow widgets for delivery by 6/8/99 with the standard 90-day warranty."

On 6/3/99, Sellco called Buyco and said that they could provide the widgets, but without any warranty. Buyco verbally agreed.

On 6/4/99 Sellco sent a written message to Buyco saying, "This is to confirm your order of 10,000 widgets with no warranty." Buyco never responded to this message or signed anything that agreed to waive the warranty.

On 6/8/99 Sellco shipped 10,000 <u>blue</u> widgets by mistake.

On 6/9/99 Buyco rejected the blue widgets and sent a letter saying, "You sent us the wrong product, you jerks. We had to buy from another supplier, and they cost us $5. You owe us $50,000."

What are the rights and remedies of the parties?

Chapter 17: Conclusion

Brilliant law students often fail to grasp that the essay grader has to grade a lot of essays in a short time. The grader just wants you to spot and state the ISSUES.

Then, for each issue the grader wants you to correctly state the AREA of law and give a good statement of the RULE that would apply to settle that particular issue.

Then for each rule, the grader wants you to identify the ELEMENTS of the rule that are supported (or not supported) by the given FACTS.

By citing FACTS, you prove the ELEMENTS. By nailing the ELEMENTS you prove the RULE. And by proving the RULE you prove the ISSUE.

When the issue is proven, just state a CONCLUSION and move on.

You MUST be prepared to recite, verbatim, certain rules of law. You do not have to memorize everything in this book, but you must be prepared to recite concise definitions and rules for some contract law concepts without hesitation. During the exam is not the time or place to begin composing a statement explaining complex legal concepts.

You don't have to be brilliant to succeed in law school. The key to success is the use of the **"Here"/"because"** word combination along with some **memorization** and plenty of **timed practices**. PRACTICING essay writing is critical so you do not run out of time.

Appendix A gives an **ALPHABETICAL LISTING** and explanation of just about **EVERY definition and rule you need to know** for CONTRACTS exams. In the rule definitions the required elements that should be the focus of your analysis are underlined for emphasis.

However, you should also read through the remaining provisions of the UCC because it is always possible the Bar Examiners will choose some obscure provision that is seldom taught or tested in law schools.[46]

Appendix B gives **SAMPLE ANSWERS** to the practice questions presented above. The word "because" appears repeatedly in the sample answers. The word "Here" addresses each ELEMENT to be proven, and the word "because" nails that element with a given FACT. That is the approach you need to learn.

Nailing the elements is the key to success in law school, and YOU WILL SUCCEED if you follow the approach presented in this book

---

[46] That is exactly what happened the June 2005 California Bar Exam for first year students where an entire question was based on UCC 2-702, which is generally considered an obscure provision.

Appendix A: Rules and Definitions for Contracts and UCC

1. **ACCEPTANCE (CONTRACTS-COMMON LAW):** Under the common law MIRROR IMAGE RULE an acceptance is an unequivocal assent to an offer, communicated to the offeror and it can be implied by silent commencement of performance known to the offeror. A response that is equivocal or contains varying terms is a REJECTION AND COUNTER-OFFER and not an effective acceptance. An offer must be accepted within a reasonable period. (see OFFER, LAPSE.)

2. **ACCEPTANCE (CONTRACTS-UCC):** Under UCC 2-206 an acceptance of an offer not other wise conditioned may be made in any REASONABLE MANNER, including a promise to ship or shipment of either conforming or non-conforming goods, but a shipment of NON-CONFORMING goods as an EXPRESS ACCOMMODATION is not an acceptance. UCC 2-207 allows an acceptance containing varying terms to be effective.

3. **ACCORD AND SATISFACTION (CONTRACTS/UCC 3-311):** An ACCORD AND SATISFACTION is a binding agreement settling a reasonable, good faith dispute over the terms and/or performance of a contract. Further, under UCC 3-311 the good faith tender and acceptance of an instrument as “full satisfaction” of any claim that is unliquidated or the subject of a bona fide dispute is generally binding, subject to certain statutory limitations and exceptions.

4. **ADHESION CONTRACT (CONTRACTS):** An adhesion contract is a "take it or leave it" offer that courts will not enforce if there is a lack of reasonable contractual intent on the part of the offeree. (see UNCONSCIONABLE CONTRACT.)

5. **ANTICIPATORY BREACH (CONTRACTS):** An anticipatory breach is a clear statement of intent by a party to a contract, prior to the time performance is due, that they will not perform when performance is due. An anticipatory breach is a MAJOR breach (see BREACH) that excuses the non-breaching party from performance and accelerates the breaching party's duty of performance to the immediate unless the non-breaching party WAIVES the breach by letting the breaching party continue performance. (compare to REASONABLE ASSURANCES.)

6. **ASSIGNMENT (CONTRACTS):** An assignment is the transfer of contractual rights from the promisee/assignor to the assignee based on a clear statement of intent by the promisee. The assignment becomes effective when the promisor is given notice of the assignment. Once the assignment is effective the promisor has a duty to deliver the benefits of the contract (pay) directly to the assignee and the rights of the original promisee/assignor are extinguished. The promisee/assignor has secondary liability to the assignee if the assignment is in exchange for consideration. (see DELEGATION.)

7. **BREACH (CONTRACTS):** A contract breach is a failure to perform a contractual duty that is currently due to be performed. It can be MAJOR or MINOR. A MAJOR breach is one that substantially deprives the non-breaching party of the EXPECTED BENEFIT OF THE BARGAIN (which see). A major breach excuses the non-breaching party from all contractual duties and waives conditions on other contractual duties of the breaching party accelerating them to become present duties. A breach is MINOR if the breaching party has

SUBSTANTIALLY PERFORMED (which see). A minor breach entitles the non-breaching party to compensation in the form of damages, but it does not excuse the non-breaching party from performance or accelerate performance by the breaching party.

8. **CONDITION CONCURRENT (CONTRACTS):** A CONDITION CONCURRENT is a condition that must be satisfied at the same time a contractual duty to perform ripens. This is rare and effectively means both parties to a contract must perform contractual duties at the same time and neither has any duty to perform unless the other party simultaneously tenders performance. (see CONDITION PRECEDENT, CONDITION SUBSEQUENT).

9. **CONDITION PRECEDENT (CONTRACTS):** A CONDITION PRECEDENT is a condition that must be satisfied before a contractual duty to perform ripens. This is very common and means that there is no contractual to perform until the condition is satisfied. (see CONDITION CONCURRENT, CONDITION SUBSEQUENT). **[Note: This term has a different meaning in real property law.]**

10. **CONDITION SUBSEQUENT (CONTRACTS):** A CONDITION SUBSEQUENT is a condition that must be satisfied while a contractual duty to perform exists, and if the condition fails the ripened duty to perform is excused. (see CONDITION CONCURRENT, CONDITION PRECEDENT). **[Note: This term has a different meaning in real property law.]**

11. **CONSEQUENTIAL DAMAGES (CONTRACTS):** Under *Hadley v. Baxendale* damages for lost profits expected from collateral contracts that fail because a contract is breached will only be awarded, absent express contract provisions otherwise, if the damages 1) were CONTEMPLATED by (known to) the breaching party at the time the contract was executed, 2) can be measured with CERTAINTY, 3) were CLEARLY CAUSED by the breach and 4) COULD NOT BE AVOIDED by the non-breaching party.

12. **CONSIDERATION (CONTRACTS):** Under contract law consideration is a bargained for exchange of value posing sufficient legal detriment that the law will enforce an agreement. Separate consideration is required to support a modification of an existing contract except under the UCC where no additional consideration is required to support contract modification.

13. **CONSTRUCTIVE CONDITIONS (CONTRACTS):** CONSTRUCTIVE CONDITIONS are implied conditions that must be satisfied before contractual duties ripen. They are implied by the nature of a contract and the express covenants within it. If a contract party promises to perform duties in exchange for payment by the other party, the duty to pay is subject to an implied CONSTRUCTIVE CONDITION PRECEDENT that the duty to pay does not ripen until the other party has completed performance. (see CONDITION PRECEDENT).

14. **CONTRACT (CONTRACTS):** A contract is a promise or set of promises, the performance of which the law recognizes as a duty and for the breach of which the law will provide a remedy.

15. **DECEIT (CONTRACTS):** Deceit is a defense to enforcement of a contract which is also called FRAUD (which see.)

16. **DEFENSE of DURESS (CONTRACTS/CRIMES):** See DURESS.

17. **DEFENSE OF MISTAKE (CONTRACTS)**: See either MUTUAL MISTAKE or UNILATERAL MISTAKE.

18. **DELEGATION (CONTRACTS):** A delegation is a transfer of contractual duties from the promisor/delegator to a delegatee based on a clear statement of intent by the delegator and acceptance of the duty by the delegatee. The promisor/delegator retains primary liability to the promisee. If the delegatee accepts contractual duties in exchange for consideration, a contract between the promisor and delegatee forms, and the promisee is an intended third party beneficiary of that contract with standing to enforce it at law against both parties. If the delegatee gratuitously accepts contractual duties the promisee can only enforce the promisor-delegatee agreement at equity based on an argument of detrimental reliance. The delegation of a contract is void if the contract requires the unique personal services or attributes of the original party, the delegator. (see ASSIGNMENT, THIRD PARTY BENEFICIARY.)

19. **DIVISIBLE CONTRACT (CONTRACTS):** Under the UCC a divisible contract is one that schedules more than one shipment of goods in a manner that payment can be made for individual shipments. Any shipment of non-conforming goods can be rejected, but a breach as to any shipment does not constitute a breach of the entire contract and does not allow the buyer to repudiate the entire contract with respect to future scheduled shipments.

20. **DURESS (CONTRACTS):** Contracts are always unenforceable against parties that enter into the agreements because of threats of physical harm, and they are generally unenforceable against parties who enter into the agreements because of threats of economic harm that were deliberately created by the party seeking to enforce the contract.

21. **ESTOPPEL (CONTRACTS):** Estoppel means that a party may be equitably barred from making a legal claim if they previously made an opposite or contradicting claim intending to induce reliance by the opposing party, and the opposing party did change position in reliance on that earlier representation. (see PROMISSORY ESTOPPEL.)

22. **EXPECTED BENEFIT OF THE BARGAIN (CONTRACTS):** The expected benefit of the bargain is the advantage or benefit that a party reasonably expects to derive from entering into a contract. (see BREACH).

23. **EXPRESS MATERIAL CONDITION (CONTRACTS):** An EXPRESS MATERIAL CONDITION is a condition that the parties to a contract expressly agreed upon, and the failure of which completely excuses a party from performance, subject to equitable considerations. (see MATERIAL CONDITIONS).

24. **FRAUD (CONTRACTS):** Fraud is a complete defense to enforcement of a contract when 1) a party seeking to enforce the contract MISREPRESENTED material facts with 2) an INTENT to DECEIVE, 3) the party seeking to void the contract REASONABLY RELIED on the misrepresented facts, and 4) the party seeking to void the contract WOULD NOT HAVE ENTERED THE CONTRACT if they had known the true facts. (Also called DECEIT; see NONDISCLOSURE as an alternative theory.)

25. **FRUSTRATION OF PURPOSE (CONTRACTS):** If a party enters into a contract knowing the specific benefit the other party seeks to gain from entering into the agreement, the continued feasibility of attaining that benefit is an IMPLIED MATERIAL CONDITION of the contract. If subsequent events beyond the control of the parties render that benefit impossible to attain, frustration of purpose causes failure of that implied material condition and the contract becomes unenforceable. (see IMPLIED MATERIAL CONDITION).

26. **GOODS (CONTRACTS):** Under the UCC goods are anything movable at the time of identification to the contract, including specially manufactured goods, unborn animals, growing crops and minerals to be removed from the land by the seller. "Goods" does not include personal property rights like copyrights, patents, stocks, bonds, or currency.

27. **ILLEGAL CONTRACT (CONTRACTS):** The court will not generally enforce a contract for a party that knowingly entered into the contract for an illegal purpose because it would impugn the integrity of the court. However, if the party seeking enforcement was not equally guilty (not IN PARI DELICTO, which see) then the court may order restitution.

28. **IMPLIED-IN-FACT CONTRACT (CONTRACTS):** If a party acts to bestow benefits on another party reasonably expecting to be paid and the other party knowingly accepts those benefits an implied-in-fact contract forms which is enforceable at law.

29. **IMPLIED-IN-LAW CONTRACT (CONTRACTS):** If a party acts to bestow benefits on another party reasonably expecting to be paid a Court of equity may hold that an implied-in-law contract has formed in order to prevent unjust enrichment to the defendant, prevent unjust detriment to the plaintiff or to protect the public interest.

30. **IMPLIED MATERIAL CONDITION (CONTRACTS):** A MATERIAL CONDITION implied by the nature of the contract. (see MATERIAL CONDITIONS).

31. **IMPOSSIBILITY (CONTRACTS):** A court will generally find there has been a failure of an IMPLIED MATERIAL CONDITION that excuses the parties from performance if performance is impossible (not just expensive or difficult) because of events that were beyond the control of the party in default. (see IMPLIED MATERIAL CONDITION).

32. **INCAPACITY (CONTRACTS):** A contract generally cannot be enforced at law against a party who lacked contractual capacity at the time of execution. If the incapacity later ends the contract will become enforceable if the party to be bound expressly RATIFIES (affirms) the contract or otherwise impliedly ratifies it by FAILING TO REPUDIATE it within a reasonable time period (often set by statute). For example, a minor may repudiate a contract at any time before reaching adulthood. If the contract is not repudiated within a reasonable time after attaining adulthood, the contract is impliedly ratified. A contract otherwise unenforceable at law based on lack of capacity may often be enforced at equity if it is for provision of necessities of life. For example, a contract for food, shelter or clothing may be enforceable against a minor at equity. (see RATIFICATION, REPUDIATION.)

33. **IN PARI DELICTO (CONTRACTS):** A court will not enforce an illegal contract or provide any restitution if the party seeking restitution is equally guilty (in pari delicto) compared to the party from whom restitution is sought.

34. **INVITATION TO NEGOTIATE (CONTRACTS):** An invitation to negotiate is any communication that fails to qualify as a contract OFFER because there is no manifestation of present contractual intent or else the terms are so vaguely stated no reasonable person would believe assent would form a bargain.

35. **LAPSE (CONTRACTS):** An offer lapses if not accepted in the time stated, or if no time is stated within a reasonable period as indicated by the means by which the offer is transmitted. An oral offer lapses at the end of the conversation. A written offer lapses at the end of the time established by the means of dispatch. Under UCC 2-205 a "firm offer" with no stated time period lapses after a reasonable time no longer than three months.

36. **LIQUIDATED DAMAGES (CONTRACTS):** A liquidated damages clause is an agreement that in the event of breach the remedy of the non-breaching party will be limited to a specified quantity of money damages. Liquidated damages clauses are unenforceable unless 1) at the time of execution the potential damages from beach were uncertain, 2) the liquidated damages specified were reasonable at the time of execution, and 3) the liquidated damages specified are reasonable at the time of breach. If a contract is for sale of UNIQUE PROPERTY money damages are inadequate and SPECIFIC PERFORMANCE is appropriate. Therefore a liquidated damages clause is unreasonable and unenforceable in such cases.

37. **LOST PROFITS (CONTRACTS):** See CONSEQUENTIAL DAMAGES.

38. **MAILBOX RULES (CONTRACTS):** Under the broadly adopted common law all contract communications are effective upon receipt by the offeror with the exception that ACCEPTANCES are generally effective upon dispatch by the offeree if they are sent by the means specified in the offer or by the same or faster means than the offer if the offer does not specify a means of communication. HOWEVER, if an offeree dispatches both an acceptance and a rejection the rejection will be effective, not the acceptance, if the rejection is received first and the offeror changes position in reliance upon it.

39. **MAJOR BREACH (CONTRACTS):** A major breach of contract is one that substantially deprives the non-breaching party of the EXPECTED BENEFIT OF THE BARGAIN. It excuses the non-breaching party from all contract duties, accelerates the duties of the breaching party, and waiving all remaining conditions on the duties of the breaching party. (see BREACH).

40. **MATERIAL CONDITION (CONTRACTS):** A MATERIAL CONDITION is one that must be satisfied for the parties to a contract to have any duty to perform. A material condition may be expressly stated by the parties or implied by the nature of the agreement. The failure of a material condition generally denies one or both parties the EXPECTED BENEFIT OF THE BARGAIN, excusing them from the contract. (see EXPECTED BENEFIT OF THE BARGAIN).

41. **MERCHANT (CONTRACTS):** Under the UCC a merchant is one who deals in or otherwise holds himself out by occupation as knowledgeable about the goods of the contract. A hobbyist can be a merchant but an occasional purchaser of goods or buyer for personal use is generally not a merchant.

42. **MUTUAL MISTAKE (CONTRACTS):** Under the common law doctrine of *Peerless*, if both parties enter into a contract because each suffers a misunderstanding of material fact the contract is void because there was no "meeting of the minds" and no valid contractual intent. (see UNILATERAL MISTAKE.)

43. **NONDISCLOSURE (CONTRACTS):** See CONCEALMENT.

44. **OFFER (CONTRACTS):** A contract offer is a manifestation of present contractual intent communicated to the offeree so certain in terms that an objective person would reasonably believe assent would form a bargain. Under common law an offer must generally specify the parties, subject matter, quantity, price, and time of performance. Under the UCC an offer must only specify the parties and quantity and the UCC "GAP FILLERS" may be used to determine additional terms. An offer LAPSES if not accepted within a reasonable period of time. (see LAPSE, ACCEPTANCE.)

45. **OPTION (CONTRACTS):** An option at common law is a contractual agreement under which an offeree exchanges consideration for a contract offer and a promise from the offeror that the offer will not be revoked for an agreed period of time. UCC 2-205 a firm offer in a signed writing by a merchant offeror that by its terms assures it will be held open for the stated time, or if no time is stated then for a reasonable time not to exceed three months, does not require consideration from the offeree.

46. **ORAL CONDITION PRECEDENT (CONTRACTS):** An ORAL CONDITION PRECEDENT is an oral agreement that a condition precedent must be satisfied or else a contractual duty to perform under the terms of a separate contract agreement will not be binding. It is an exception to the PAROL EVIDENCE RULE. (see PAROL EVIDENCE RULE, CONDITION PRECEDENT.)

47. **PAROL EVIDENCE RULE (CONTRACTS):** Evidence concerning PRIOR or CONTEMPORANEOUS agreements can not be introduced to VARY or CONTRADICT the terms of a FULLY INTEGRATED WRITING unless they are offered to show evidence of **[DAM FOIL]** Duress, Ambiguity, Mistake, Fraud, Oral condition precedent, Illegality, or Lack of consideration.

48. **PERFECT TENDER RULE (CONTRACTS):** Under the UCC goods must be delivered in complete conformity with the contractual agreement and any NON-CONFORMING delivery can be rejected by the buyer. In effect, every breach is treated as a major breach because buyers are released from their legal duties.

49. **PROMISSORY ESTOPPEL (CONTRACTS):** Promissory estoppel is an equitable doctrine barring a party from revoking a promise if 1) the party made a promise, 2) intending to induce or reasonably knowing that it would induce reliance, 3) there was reasonable reliance by the other party seeking enforcement of the promise, and 4) injustice would result otherwise. (see ESTOPPEL).

50. **QUANTUM MERUIT (CONTRACTS):** Quantum meruit is used by different people to mean different things. Generally it is used to mean RESTITUTION or the award of damages in restitution to prevent UNJUST ENRICHMENT (which see). But this term is also used at times to mean an implied-in-law contract or even implied contracts in general.

51. **RATIFICATION (CONTRACTS):** Ratification is the act of contract parties who lack contractual capacity at the time of execution (e.g. minors) affirming otherwise voidable contracts after attaining contractual capacity. (see INCAPACITY, REPUDIATION.)

52. **REASONABLE ASSURANCES (CONTRACTS):** A contract party that has reasonable doubts about the other party's ability or willingness to perform future duties under a contract may demand REASONABLE ASSURANCES from the other party in the form of a financial guarantee or payment to escrow. A failure to provide reasonable assurances may be treated as an anticipatory repudiation of the contract.

53. **REMEDY OF NON-BREACHING BUYER (CONTRACTS):** A non-breaching buyer may invoke SPECIFIC PERFORMANCE (which see) to obtain possession and title to unique property such as LAND but not personal services. Otherwise, the non-breaching party can demand damages equal to the EXPECTED BENEFIT OF THE BARGAIN (which see). Under the UCC a non-breaching buyer may also ACCEPT or REJECT non-conforming goods, REPUDIATE the contract and COVER by purchase of conforming goods or AFFIRM the contract and DEMAND DELIVERY of conforming goods.

54. **REMEDY OF NON-BREACHING SELLER (CONTRACTS):** A non-breaching seller may generally demand damages equal to the EXPECTED BENEFIT OF THE BARGAIN (which see). Under the UCC the non-breaching seller has four remedies: 1) If the goods can be sold at market price the seller may demand the excess of the CONTRACT PRICE over the MARKET PRICE. 2) Otherwise, the goods may be sold at a SALVAGE sale after NOTICE to the breaching buyer, and the seller can demand the excess of the CONTRACT PRICE over the SALVAGE PRICE. 3) In a LOST VOLUME situation where the seller cannot easily resell the goods to other customers the seller can demand LOST PROFITS. 4) If the goods are custom made or otherwise unsuitable for sale to other customers the seller can demand payment of the CONTRACT PRICE (specific performance).

55. **REMEDY OF BREACHING BUYER (CONTRACTS):** A breaching buyer may obtain RETURN OF DEPOSITS paid to the non-breaching seller in RESTITUTION to the extent they exceed the seller's damages.

56. **REMEDY OF BREACHING SELLER (CONTRACTS):** At common law a seller that substantially performs has a right to be paid the contract price less an offset for damages. A seller that has committed a major breach may still obtain EQUITABLE RESTITUTION (quantum meruit reimbursement) to prevent unjust enrichment to the extent their performance conferred benefits on the non-breaching buyer. Under the UCC the breaching seller can give notice of intent to cure and has a right to cure during the contract period. The breaching seller also has a REASONABLE RIGHT FOR EXTRA TIME TO CURE their shipment of non-conforming goods if they shipped them with a reasonable belief they were suitable for the buyer's needs.

57. **REPUDIATION (CONTRACTS):** The act of a party lacking capacity declaring a contract void. (see INCAPACITY, RATIFICATION.)

58. **RESTITUTION (CONTRACTS):** Restitution is an award of damages to the plaintiff to restore the STATUS QUO or prevent UNJUST ENRICHMENT by the defendant (which see).

59. **REVOCATION (CONTRACTS):** A revocation is a withdrawal or cancellation of an offer by the offeror, and it is effective if received by the offeree before the offer has been effectively accepted. An offeror cannot revoke an option contract for the time agreed as long as the option contract is properly supported by consideration. Under modern SAVING DOCTRINES a UNILATERAL CONTRACT OFFER may not be revocable if the offeror is aware the offeree has commenced performance of the requested act (see SAVING DOCTRINES)..

60. **SAVING DOCTRINES (CONTRACTS):** Under the modern view a UNILATERAL CONTRACT OFFER generally cannot be revoked if the offeror is aware the offeree has commenced performance of the requested act necessary for acceptance until the offeree has been given a reasonable time to complete performance. Some States allow revocation but require restitution to prevent unjust enrichment.

61. **SPECIFIC PERFORMANCE (CONTRACTS):** If money damages are an inadequate legal remedy because unique property (land, art objects, etc.) are in dispute a Court of equity may order enforcement of a contract promise.

62. **STANDING (CONTRACTS):** Standing means that a plaintiff has a right to pursue a legal remedy because they have suffered actual damages.

63. **STATUS QUO (CONTRACTS):** The status quo means the positions of the parties prior to entering into a contract agreement.

64. **STATUTE OF FRAUDS (CONTRACTS):** Under the Statute of Frauds certain contracts, otherwise valid, cannot be enforced unless supported by a writing. The contracts affected are those for MARRIAGE, those that would necessarily take more than a YEAR to complete, those for the conveyance of an interest in LAND, those by an EXECUTOR of an estate, those for the GUARANTEE of a debt. **[MYLEG]** The rule on the sale of goods is modernly superceded by the UCC. See UCC 2-201.

65. **SUBSTANTIAL PERFORMANCE (CONTRACTS):** Substantial performance means that a breaching contract party substantially provided the non-breaching party with the EXPECTED BENEFIT OF THE BARGAIN (which see.)

66. **THIRD PARTY BENEFICIARY (CONTRACTS):** A person who is intended to receive benefits under a contract between two other parties has STANDING to enforce the contract and seek damages for breach if they are vested. Modernly it does not matter if the original contract parties acted to extinguish a debt to the third party (CREDITOR beneficiaries) or acted out of gratuitous motives (DONEE beneficiaries). The third party beneficiary may enforce the contract after they vest by becoming aware of and relying on the existence of the contract. A party that benefits from a contract that was not established for their benefit

is an INCIDENTAL beneficiary with no standing to enforce, even if they have relied on the contract's existence.

67. **UCC (CONTRACTS):** Article 2 of the Uniform Commercial Code controls contracts for the sale of GOODS.

68. **UCC 1-206 (CONTRACTS):** A contract for the sale of personal property that is not goods (e.g. patents, recording rights) worth more than $5,000 must be in writing, signed by the party to be bound, identifying the subject matter and defining or stating a price.

69. **UCC 2-201 (CONTRACTS):** A contract for goods worth $500 or more must be in writing, signed by the party against whom the contract is to be enforced. This limit is currently being raised to $5,000 but many States still use the $500 limit. But between merchants a SALES CONFIRMATION by one listing quantity will bind both parties if the receiving party does not object within 10 days. Further, the rule does not apply to CUSTOM MADE GOODS, where there is an ADMISSION by the party to be bound in a legal setting that there had been an agreement, or where there has been PARTIAL PERFORMANCE of the contract by acceptance of payment or goods.

70. **UCC 2-205 (CONTRACTS):** A firm offer in a signed writing by a merchant that by its terms assures it will be held open creates an OPTION that does not require consideration for the stated time, or, if no time is stated in the contract, for a reasonable time not to exceed three months. (see OPTION.)

71. **UCC 2-206 (CONTRACTS):** An acceptance may be made in any REASONABLE MANNER, including a promise to ship or shipment of either conforming or non-conforming goods, but a shipment of NON-CONFORMING goods as an EXPRESS ACCOMMODATION is not an acceptance.

72. **UCC 2-207 (CONTRACTS):** An acceptance containing varying terms is an effective acceptance, but the varying terms will NOT be included in the contract if 1) the offer expressly limited acceptance and the offeror does not agree to the new terms, OR 2) the parties are not both merchants, OR 3) the varying terms materially alter the contract OR 4) the party to be bound objects within a reasonable period of time.

73. **UNCONSCIONABLE CONTRACT (CONTRACTS):** A Court will not enforce a contract that is so one-sided that it implies a lack of reasonable intent to be bound on the part of the offeree. (see ADHESION contract.)

74. **UNIFORM COMMERCIAL CODE (CONTRACTS):** see UCC.

75. **UNILATERAL CONTRACT (CONTRACTS):** A unilateral contract offer is one that by its own terms unequivocally restricts the means of acceptance to the act of complete performance only. (See SAVING DOCTRINES).

76. **UNILATERAL MISTAKE (CONTRACTS):** Under contract law if a party enters into a contract suffering from a misunderstanding of fact that the other party knew or should have known about, the contract is voidable by the mistaken party. But if the other party did not know or have reason to know of the mistake the contract is legally binding and not

voidable in most States. In a minority of States the mistaken party may rescind the contract if 1) the error is discovered before the other party has irrevocably acted in reliance, 2) prompt notice of the error is given, and 3) the other party is reimbursed for all expenses caused by the error and rescission. (see MUTUAL MISTAKE.)

77. **UNJUST ENRICHMENT (CONTRACTS):** A Court may award damages in RESTITUTION to prevent an unjust enrichment. (see RESTITUTION).

78. **WAIVER OF BREACH (CONTRACTS):** A "waiver of a breach" is an ELECTION by a non-breaching party to treat a major breach as a minor breach, allowing the breaching party to continue performing under the contract. Following the waiver of a breach the non-breaching party cannot retract the waiver to claim a major breach.

79. **WAIVER OF CONDITION (CONTRACTS):** A waiver of condition means that a contract party performs a contractual duty that was not due to be performed because it was subject to a CONDITION PRECEDENT that was not satisfied. Following a waiver of a condition the performing party may retract the waiver and refuse to perform the duty in the future unless the condition is satisfied.

Appendix B: Sample Answers

The sample answers are presented in *italics*. An answer explanation follows each.

Sample Answer 16-1: Contract Formation

HOMER v. LUCY

The rights and remedies of the parties depend on whether or not there was a valid contract. A contract is a promise or set of promises the performance of which the law will recognize as a duty and for which the law will provide a remedy.

1) UCC?

UCC Article 2 governs contracts for the sale of GOODS, movable things at the time of identification to the contract. Otherwise, only COMMON LAW governs the contract.

Here the contract does not concern a sale of movable things because it is for the "rent" of a "house".

Therefore, only COMMON LAW principles govern this contract.

2) Is a WRITING REQUIRED?

Under the STATUTE OF FRAUDS certain types of contracts must be in writing to be enforced. A contract for conveyance of an interest in LAND often requires a writing, but not leaseholds of a year or less.

Here the question involves conveyance of an interest in land because the alleged agreement was to rent a "house", but this appears to be a month-to-month rental.

Therefore, a writing would not generally be required.

3) Was the ADVERTISEMENT an OFFER?

Under contract law an OFFER is a manifestation of present intent to enter into a bargain communicated to the offeree and sufficiently specific that an observer would reasonably believe assent would form a bargain. Advertisements are generally not offers because they usually fail to identify the parties or the quantity being offered.

Here the advertisement was not specific as to the parties because it did not guarantee that Lucy would rent to the first person to respond.

Therefore, the advertisement was not an offer.

4) <u>Was the 9:00 statement by Homer an OFFER?</u>

Offer is defined above.

Here the statement by Homer did not appear to <u>manifest intent</u> to enter into a bargain because even though he said, "I accept" he added that he "had to see the house first." No reasonable person would believe assent to that statement would form a bargain because it was clear he wanted to "see the house first."

Therefore the statement was not an offer.

5) <u>Was the 9:00 response by Lucy an OFFER?</u>

Offer is defined above.

Here the statement by Lucy did <u>manifest intent</u> to enter into a bargain because she said "It's a deal. I will rent to you for $550." A reasonable person would believe assent to that statement would form a bargain.

Therefore that statement was an offer.

6) <u>Did Homer have a valid OPTION?</u>

Offer is defined above. Under common law an OPTION is a contractual agreement that an offeror will not revoke an offer for a specific period of time <u>in exchange for CONSIDERATION</u> from the offeree. CONSIDERATION is an exchange of promises posing <u>legal detriment</u> such that the law deems it sufficient to support an agreement.

Here Lucy promised to give a "firm offer", but Homer <u>gave no promise or value in exchange.</u> While the UCC provides for "firm offers" from merchants, the UCC does not govern here. Therefore, Lucy received no legal consideration in exchange for her promise to give a "firm offer" and her promise cannot be enforced against her as an option contract.

Therefore, Lucy's offer did not create an option contract, and she could revoke her offer at any time.

7) <u>Did Homer effectively ACCEPT at 3:00?</u>

At common law an acceptance must be an unequivocal assent to the terms of an offer, dispatched to the offeror in the manner required, or if no manner is required in the offer, by the means by which the offer was dispatched or some faster means.. An offer must be accepted before it LAPSES. Unless there is an option, an offer lapses in the <u>time stated</u> or if no time is stated within a <u>reasonable time</u> after the offer is made.

Here the reasonable time for acceptance of Lucy's offer is defined by the understanding that Homer would view the house in only one hour at "10:00". That understanding established the "reasonable time" within which Homer could accept the offer. But Homer was "five hours late," so Lucy's offer had already lapsed when he arrived. Homer's attempt to unequivocally accept Lucy's 9:00 offer by saying "I unequivocally accept" was ineffective because he could not accept an offer that had already lapsed.

Therefore, Homer's attempt to accept was ineffective.

[**ANSWER EXPLANATION:** This question is a typical FORMATION question because it goes through a series of communications between the parties. When you see messages going back and forth, it is a FORMATION question, so analyze each message.

Start with an INTRODUCTORY DEFINITION of a contract. Then chronologically analyze each communication to see if it is an OFFER. Once there is an offer, the next issue is whether the offer is ACCEPTED.

If there is offer and an acceptance a contract forms and the next issue is the TERMS of the contract.

After the contract and terms are discussed the next issue is whether there has been a BREACH. And if there is a breach, the issues are WHO BREACHED and the REMEDIES of the parties.]

Sample Answer 16-2: UCC and Acceptance Varying Terms

BOB v. AL

The rights and remedies of the parties here depend on whether there was a valid contract. A CONTRACT is a promise or set of promises the performance of which the law will recognize as a duty and for the breach of which the law will provide a remedy.

1) UCC?

Article 2 of the UCC governs contracts for the sale of GOODS, movable things at the time of identification to the contract.

Here the contract is for sale of a moveable thing because it was for sale of a "tuxedo".

Therefore this was a contract for a sale of goods and the UCC governs.

2) MERCHANTS?

Under the UCC MERCHANTS are people who deal in the goods or hold themselves out by occupation as knowledgeable about the goods in a contract.

Here Bob deals in tuxedos because he has a clothing store. Al may have "bought a lot of clothes " but there is no evidence he deals in tuxedos or hold himself out by occupation as being particularly knowledgeable about them.

Therefore Bob is a merchant and Al is not.

3) Is A WRITING NEEDED?

Under UCC 2-201 a contract for the sale of GOODS over $500 requires a writing. This limit is being raised to $5,000 but many States are still using the $500 limit. Under the UCC a contract between MERCHANTS may satisfy the need for a writing against both parties if there is a sales confirmation indicating the quantity sent to one party by the other and the receiving party does not object to the representation of a contract.

Further, under the UCC there is no need for a writing if goods are custom made, the person to be bound acknowledges the contract in a legal setting or where a party has accepted payment or goods.

Here the goods are over $500 because the tuxedo costs "$519.95." And Al is not a merchant as shown above.

Further, this was a "ready-made" tuxedo, not custom made, and Al never acknowledged the contract in a legal setting or accepted the goods.

Therefore a writing signed by Al is needed if the contract is to be enforced against him by Bob.

4) Did Bob OFFER to sell the tuxedo?

Under contract law an OFFER is a manifestation of present contractual intent communicated to the offeree that is so specific that an objective observer would reasonably believe assent would form a bargain.

Here Bob manifested an intent to sell a tuxedo because he "suggested Al buy" the tuxedo. And a reasonable person would believe assent to this communication would form a bargain.

Therefore, Bob made an offer.

5) Did Al ACCEPT Bob's offer?

Under the UCC acceptance of an offer can be made by any reasonable means showing assent to an offer.

Here Al showed assent by a reasonable means because he " agreed".

Therefore, Al accepted Bob's offer.

6) What were the TERMS of the bargain?

Under the UCC the subject matter, quantity and parties must be specified for a contract to be sufficiently certain, but all other terms can be supplied by the UCC's GAP FILLERS.

Here the parties are Al and Bob and the subject matter is one tuxedo that is to be "exactly Al's size." Although price was not agreed upon that term would be inferred by the normal price for such goods. If $519.95 was the normal price of the tuxedo, it would be the price supplied by the UCC. The place of delivery was Bob's store and the time of delivery was agreed to be "later in the week."

Therefore the TERMS of the contract were sufficiently certain for it to be enforced.

7) BREACH?

Under the UCC PERFECT TENDER RULE goods must be delivered exactly as ordered. A seller that gives notice of intent to CURE a shipment of non-conforming goods has a right to cure within the contract period and a right to extra time to cure if non-conforming goods were delivered with a reasonable belief they were suitable for the buyer's needs.

Here Bob delivered non-conforming goods because the tuxedo was not an "exact fit" as promised. Bob gave notice of intent to cure, and had time within the contract period to cure the lack of fit.

Therefore, Bob breached, but had a right to cure the breach.

Was the contract MODIFIED to a higher price?

Under the UCC a modification of a contract by agreement between the parties does not require additional consideration.

Here Al did not agree to pay a higher price because he only "nodded" agreement to the need for alterations. The alterations were so that Bob could cure his breach, and while Bob has a right to cure his breach, he has no right to charge Al for the alterations. Further, Al did not agree to modify the original contract terms.

Therefore, the contract was not modified to a higher price.

8) Can Al raise the LACK OF WRITING as a defense?

As discussed above, Bob could not enforce the contract unless he had a signed writing from Al.

No facts show that Al ever signed any writing to buy the tuxedo.

Therefore, Bob cannot force Al to pay for the tuxedo.

9) FRUSTRATION OF PURPOSE?

Under contract law, if the parties enter into a contract knowing that the failure of some condition beyond their control will deny one of the parties the benefit of the bargain, that condition is an implied material condition of the contract, the failure of which excuses both parties from the agreement.

Here Bob knew that if the wedding of Al's daughter was cancelled it would deny Al the benefit of the bargain because he wanted the tuxedo to "wear to the wedding."

Therefore, Al can claim frustration of purpose excuses him from the contract.

[**ANSWER EXPLANATION:** This is a UCC question, obviously. Bob breached by delivering non-conforming goods that failed to provide a perfect fit, as promised. But he has time to cure, and gave notice he intended to cure.

If Al wants out of the deal, he can claim a lack of a writing. He can do that because he is not a merchant, and the "sales confirmation" does not apply to him. He would be a merchant if he were a collector or hobbyist. But just buying lots of clothes doesn't make him a merchant any more than you are a merchant because you have bought a lot of groceries.

And Al also possibly can claim frustration of purpose.]

Sample Answer 16-3: Third Parties in a UCC Setting

The rights and remedies of the parties here depend on whether there was a valid contract. A CONTRACT is a promise or set of promises the performance of which the law will recognize as a duty and for the breach of which the law will provide a remedy.

1) UCC?

UCC Article 2 governs contracts for the sale of GOODS, movable things at the time of identification to the contract.

Here the question involves a sale of a "car" and it is movable because it was to be delivered.

Therefore, the UCC applies here.

GROUCHO v. HARPO

2) Groucho's rights under a THIRD-PARTY BENEFICIARY CONTRACT?

Under contract law a THIRD-PARTY BENEFICIARY CONTRACT is one with a main purpose of providing a benefit to a third party. The contract can be enforced by the original party, the promisee, or by a vested intended beneficiary.

A beneficiary may be a DONEE (of a gift) or a CREDITOR (payment of a debt) beneficiary. The beneficiary vests upon becoming aware of and changing position in reliance on the contract.

Here the purpose of the contract is to benefit Chico because he was to get a "new Dodge" as a "birthday present." Therefore this is a third-party benefit contract. Chico is an intended DONEE beneficiary because it is a "birthday present."

Groucho is the promisee because Harpo promised to "deliver" the car in "two weeks." Harpo is the promisor because he has promised to deliver the car to Chico.

Therefore, this is a third-party beneficiary contract, and Groucho as promisee can enforce it.

3) Groucho's REMEDIES?

Under the PERFECT TENDER RULE of the UCC a non-breaching buyer in a non-delivery situation can demand conforming goods, repudiate the contract or by goods to cover and demand the excess of the cover price over the contract price.

Here Harpo has breached because he did not deliver the promised car.

Therefore, Groucho can demand delivery from Harpo or repudiate the contract and demand return of his $2,000. If he covers by buying the car elsewhere he can demand the excess of his cover price, if any, over the contract price.

GROUCHO v. SWIFTY

4) Groucho's rights under the DELEGATION contract?

Under contract law a DELEGATION is a second contract conveying the duty of performance under the first contract from the original promisor to a delegatee. The promisor in the first contract retains primary liability to the promisee. The delegatee assumes secondary liability to the promisee of the first contract if she expressly accepts the delegation in exchange for consideration, a bargained for exchange of value creating legal liability. In the delegation contract between the promisor/delegator and the delegatee the original promisee is a CREDITOR third-party beneficiary with standing to enforce the contract.

A delegatee can raise all defenses that are available to the promisee in the original contract.

Here there is a delegation contract between Harpo and Swifty supported by consideration because Swifty expressly accepted the duty by saying he "agreed to deliver" in exchange for an "immediate payment of $20,000".

Therefore, Groucho has standing to enforce Swifty's promise to deliver the car as a creditor third-party beneficiary.

5) Groucho's REMEDIES against Swifty?

A promisee under a contract can enforce the delegation contract as an intended third-party beneficiary in the same way as the original promisee of the delegation agreement (Harpo).

Here Groucho's remedies against Swifty are the same as his remedies against Harpo, and Groucho can recover from Swifty any amounts he cannot recover from Harpo.

HARPO v. SWIFTY

6) Harpo's rights under the DELEGATION contract?

Delegation is defined above.

Here the delegation from Harpo to Swifty is a contract between them because Swifty promised "to deliver the car", and it is a legal contract supported by consideration because Swifty received an "immediate payment of $20,000".Swifty was the promisor and Harpo the promisee.

Therefore, Harpo can enforce his contract with Swifty and seek recovery from Swifty for any damages due Groucho and/or Chico.

CHICO v. HARPO

7) *Chico's rights as a THIRD-PARTY BENEFICIARY?*

Third-party beneficiary contracts are defined above. Chico is an intended third-party beneficiary because the known purpose of the original contract was to give him a "birthday present." He vested when he became aware of the original contract and changed position in reliance.

A vested third-party beneficiary can enforce the contract against the promisor in the same manner as the promisee.

Therefore, Chico can enforce the original contract against Harpo in the same manner and extent as Groucho

8) *Chico's REMEDIES?*

Chico's remedies would be the same as Groucho.

CHICO v. SWIFTY

9) *Chico's rights and remedies against Swifty?*

Since Swifty agreed to perform the duties of Harpo, Swifty assumed the same liability as Harpo. And since Chico has the same enforcement rights as Groucho, Chico's rights and remedies to enforce the contract against Swifty are the same as against Harpo.

CHICO v. GROUCHO

10) *Chico's rights and remedies against Groucho?*

A donee beneficiary cannot enforce the promise of a gift against the promisee at law and can only enforce at equity based on promissory estoppel.

Here Groucho entered into the contract with Harpo to give Chico a GIFT, so Chico was a DONEE beneficiary. While there is no evidence Groucho has breached the contract with Harpo, and even if he did Chico would have no right to enforce the contract against Groucho at law.

Therefore, if Groucho had refused to perform the contract (e.g. had refused to make the car payments) Chico could only plead equity against Groucho based on principals of promissory estoppel.

[**ANSWER EXPLANATION:** The point of this question is that a contract intended to benefit a third party (Chico) can be enforced against the promisor (Harpo) by both the intended beneficiary (Chico) and the promisee (Groucho). Further, a delegation contract supported by consideration (a legally binding contract and not just a gift promise) can be enforced by the delegator (Harpo) against the delegatee (Swifty) and also by the promisee (Groucho) and intended beneficiary (Chico).

But if the promisee's effort (Groucho's effort) to bestow benefit on the beneficiary (Chico) is gratuitous, the donee beneficiary cannot enforce the original contract (Groucho-Harpo contract) against the promisee (Groucho) at law. The donee beneficiary could only plead promissory estoppel or detrimental reliance against the promisee in equity, given evidence to support such a claim.

If the contract is for a sale of goods, as is the case here, the UCC also governs the remedies of the parties at law, but the equitable remedies would generally remain the same as at common law.

You should identify each party as promisee, promisor, delegatee, donee/creditor beneficiary, etc. because that designation determines their RIGHTS and REMEDIES (just as the call of the question asks.)

Keeping the parties straight may require drawing a diagram and labeling each party with the various terms.]

Sample Answer 16-4: Defenses

TOM v. AL

1. *Was the contract of January 1 unenforceable by Tom because it was oral?*

1) UCC?

UCC Article 2 governs the sale of goods, moveable things at the time of identification to the contract. But UCC Article 1 generally requires a written contract signed by the party to be bound for any sale of personal property that is not goods in excess of $5,000.

Here Tom claimed the records were "goods" but the contract was not for the sale of anything movable because it was for the sale of "recording rights". But it was for a sale of personal property because it was for "exclusive recording rights." The value of the contract was not stated to be over $5,000, and it might be argued that on that basis Article I would not require a writing at the time of execution, even though the song later became popular.

Therefore UCC Article 2 would not require this contract to be in writing, and it is arguable that Article 1 would not require a writing because the contract was not clearly in excess of $5,000 at the time of execution.

2) Statute of Frauds?

Under the STATUTE OF FRAUDS a contract that necessarily takes more than a year to complete from the time of formation must be in writing to be enforceable at law. But if an oral agreement that fails to satisfy the statute is partially or fully performed, it may be enforceable at equity to the extent necessary to prevent injustice. To plead equity one must have "clean hands".

Here the contract would necessarily take more than a year because it was entered "two days before" Al was 17 and it was to last until he was "18". That is more than a year.

Therefore, the Statute of Frauds required a writing even if Article 1 of the UCC did not. Al only agreed to the contract orally, so and the contract was not enforceable against him at law because it was oral.

Further, Tom would be unable to plead "clean hands" because he appears to have taken advantage of Al, a minor, and to have lied to Deccra about Al's age.

Therefore Tom would be unable to enforce the oral agreement against Al at either law or equity.

2. Was the contract of January 1 enforceable against Tom by Al?

3) STATUTE OF FRAUDS?

The Statute of Frauds is defined above.

Here Tom sent Al a "signed" confirmation that "gave all the details". And Al also has "performed completely".

Therefore there may be sufficient "writing" signed by Tom that the Statue of Frauds might be satisfied.

Otherwise Al would probably be able to enforce the contract against Tom at equity to the extent necessary to avoid injustice.

4) Enforceable by a MINOR?

Under contract law a contract, except for necessities of life, cannot be enforced at law against a party which lacked legal capacity at the time of execution. But if a legal incapacity is removed the party to be bound must repudiate the contract within a reasonable period of time or they will be deemed to have affirmed or ratified it. The period of time in which a party gaining legal capacity must repudiate a contract may be set by statue.

A party lacking capacity can enforce a contract against a party that does not lack capacity.

Here Al lacked capacity at the time of execution because it was "two days before his seventeenth birthday". But that does not prevent Al from enforcing the contract against Tom who did not lack capacity.

Therefore the contract is enforceable by Al, even though he is a minor.

AL v. DECCRA

3. Was the contract of March 1 enforceable by Al against Deccra?

5) FRAUD?

Under contract law FRAUD is a defense to enforcement of a contract where a party 1) deliberately misrepresented material facts, 2) the party raising the defense reasonably relied on the misrepresentations, and 3) the party to be bound would not have entered into the contract but for the misrepresentation.

Here Tom deliberately misrepresented facts because he said Al was "19" knowing that Al was a minor. And this was a material fact since it represented Al had legal capacity to enter into a contract. And Decca reasonably relied on Tom's misrepresentation, and could probably prove it would not have entered the contract had it known the truth.

Therefore, the contract of March 1 was unenforceable against Deccra.

4. ISSUE -- Was the contract of April 1 enforceable by Deccra against Al?

6) EFFECTIVE REPUDIATION OF CONTRACT?

As explained above a contract, except for necessities of life, cannot be enforced against a party lacking legal capacity at the time of execution. But if a party lacking capacity at the time of contract gains capacity, they must affirmatively repudiate the contract within a reasonable period of time, or within the time set by statute, or they will be deemed to have affirmed or ratified the contract.

Here Al lacked capacity to contract at the time of execution because he was a <u>minor</u> who was "only 17".

Al later attempted to repudiate the contract "six months after becoming an adult." He would argue that this was within a "reasonable" time after he gained capacity. And if this was within the statutory time period the repudiation was effective. Otherwise the contract may have been deemed automatically affirmed and the repudiation would be ineffective.

If the repudiation was effective, Decca would generally be required to give to Al all money it had made on the sale of his song.

Therefore, Deccra cannot enforce the contract if Al's repudiation was effective.

<u>5. If the contract of April 1 is legally unenforceable by Deccra, what equitable argument might it make?</u>

<u>7) PROMISSORY ESTOPPEL?.</u>

Under the doctrine of PROMISSORY ESTOPPEL a party can seek enforcement of an otherwise unenforceable promise where 1) a party <u>made a promise</u>, 2) <u>intending to induce reliance</u>, 3) there was <u>reasonable reliance</u> by the other party and 4) <u>injustice</u> will result if the promise is not enforced..

Here Al <u>made a promise</u> to Deccra because he "agreed on April 1 to a new arrangement", and he did that <u>intending to induce reliance</u>.

Al would argue that Decca did not <u>reasonably rely</u> because it was <u>aware</u> Al was a minor and could repudiate the contract at any time. Deccra would argue that Al would reap an UNJUST ENRICHMENT because it incurred "$360,000 in distribution expense."

Therefore, it would appear that Decca's restitution to Al should be reduced by this amount and restricted to the actual profit made by Decca.

[**ANSWER EXPLANATION:** The most important thing this question teaches is how to "follow the call" of a STRUCTURED CALL while still addressing important issues the call fails to mention.

While the CALL asks you about Tom's rights against Al, and Al's rights against Tom, and Al's rights against Deccra, and Deccra's rights against Al, you only have to state the parties twice: "Tom v. Al" and "Al v. Deccra". It is simply a waste of time to state the parties again with their names switched around.

The call of the question asks the validity of an oral contract. That requires you to immediately determine if the UCC applies. UCC Article 2 does not apply because this question does not involve the sale of goods, but Article 1 (1-206) may apply because it involves a sale of recording rights. Even if those do not apply, the Statute of Frauds applies because this is a contract that necessarily cannot be performed in less than a year.

Remember oral contracts and contracts signed by minors may be valid but not enforceable. Or, they may be unenforceable at law but enforceable at equity. It depends on the facts. Even if a party cannot enforce the contract, they may get quantum meruit reimbursement if the other party would otherwise receive an unjust enrichment.

Deccra's defense against enforcement of the March 1 contract could be stated as the issue of "unilateral mistake" where Tom knew Deccra was mistaken, but since Tom deliberately lied to Deccra about Al's age with intent to deceive "fraud" seems the more accurate issue statement.]

Sample Answer 16-5: Common Law Modification, Breach and Remedy

WANDA v. HOMER

The rights and remedies of the parties here depend on whether there was a valid contract. A CONTRACT is a promise or set of promises the performance of which the law will recognize as a duty and for the breach of which the law will provide a remedy.

1) UCC?

Article 2 of the UCC governs contracts for the sale of GOODS. GOODS are movable things at the time of identification to the contract. Otherwise only the common law applies.

Here the contract does not involve a sale because it is a contract for personal services -- building a house.

Therefore, only the COMMON LAW applies.

2) Is a WRITING REQUIRED?

Under the STATUTE OF FRAUDS certain types of contracts must be in writing to be enforced. A contract for conveyance of an interest in LAND generally requires a writing, and contracts that necessarily must take more than a year to complete require a writing.

Here the contract is for building a house, and does not involve conveyance of an interest in land because Homer "already owns" the land. And the contract can be performed in less than a year because it was to be completed before the "Winter rains".

Therefore, no writing is required by the Statute of Frauds

3) MODIFICATION without CONSIDERATION?

Under COMMON LAW a contract modification must be supported by CONSIDERATION, a bargained for exchange of value posing legal detriment sufficient to enforce the modification at law.

Here the contract was modified because Homer promised to pay $30,000 more. But Bill did not give anything of value in exchange for that promise since he only agreed to do what he already had a PRE-EXISTING DUTY to do -- to build the house for $100,000.

Therefore, the modification of the contract was not supported by consideration and it is unenforceable at law against Homer.

4) <u>Enforceable by PROMISSORY ESTOPPEL?</u>

Under the theory of PROMISSORY ESTOPPEL an agreement that otherwise is unenforceable at law for a lack of consideration may be enforced at equity to the extent necessary to avoid injustice. In order to plead equity a party must have CLEAN HANDS. Promissory estoppel applies where the party to be bound made a 1) <u>promise</u> with 2) <u>intent to induce reliance</u> and there 3) was <u>reasonable reliance</u> and 4) failure to enforce the promise would cause an <u>injustice</u>.

Here Homer made a <u>promise</u> because he "promised" to pay $30,000. And he did that with <u>intent to induce reliance</u> because Homer didn't want to "live in a tent". Bill <u>reasonably relied</u> on Homer's promise because he "hired Fred" in "reasonable reliance" on the promise. But there is <u>NO INJUSTICE</u> because Bill was only induced by Homer's lie to do exactly what he was already legally obligated to do -- finish the house. Homer reaped NO UNJUST ENRICHMENT because he only got the house that he had already been promised, and had promised to pay for.

Therefore, Bill was not induced to do anything he was not otherwise obligated to do, and Homer did not receive anything of value that he was not entitled to.

Since there was <u>no injustice</u>, promissory estoppel would not apply.

Further, Bill had UNCLEAN HANDS because he had a <u>legal duty</u> to perform under the contract, and he elicited Homer's promise to pay $30,000 more by <u>threatening to breach</u> the contract. A Court of equity will not act to enforce a promise elicited by a threat of illegal conduct.

Therefore, Homer's promise to pay more cannot be enforced at either law or equity.

5) <u>Defense of IMPOSSIBILITY?</u>

Under contract law the defense of IMPOSSIBILITY excuses a breach where the performance of a contract has become <u>impossible</u> due to events <u>beyond the control of the parties</u>. Impossibility means that performance is physically impossible, and it constitutes a failure of an IMPLIED MATERIAL CONDITION of the agreement.

Here finishing the house was <u>not impossible</u> because Homer finished it by hiring Paul.

Therefore, Wanda cannot claim impossibility as a defense.

6) <u>BREACH?</u>

Under contract law a BREACH is a failure to perform contractual duties when they become due. A MAJOR BREACH is one which denies the non-breaching party the <u>EXPECTED BENEFIT OF THE BARGAIN</u>. A major breach completely excuses the non-breaching party from any further obligation under the contract. A MINOR BREACH is one where the breaching party has <u>SUBSTANTIALLY PERFORMED</u>. When there is a minor breach the non-breaching party must perform contractual duties but is entitled to an OFFSET as compensation for damages.

Here there was substantial performance because the home was all done "except for the painting". The minor breach cost Homer an additional $10,000, so he was entitled to an OFFSET in that amount.

Therefore, Homer must pay Wanda the contract price less an offset of $10,000, a net payment of $90,000.

[**ANSWER EXPLANATION:** Don't let sympathy blind you. Effective modification of a common law contract (not UCC) requires an exchange of consideration. Here Bill receives a promise of $30,000, but Homer gets nothing. If Homer gets nothing, then he gets no consideration (no bargained for thing in exchange for his promise).

Restatement 2nd provides that a "good faith" modification requires no consideration to be enforced at law. But that is not clearly "broadly adopted". The general view seems to be that consideration is required to enforce a modification agreement at law, and without consideration it may only be enforced at equity to the extent necessary to avoid injustice. Besides, an agreement made "under threat" is hardly in good faith anyway.

Consider a situation where Bill demands $30,000 more but also promises to paint the house a different color. In that case there would be a bargained for exchange of consideration, so Homer would have to argue he was forced to agree to pay more under duress, a different legal defense argument. But here that is not the case, so any argument of 'duress' is unnecessary and irrelevant.

For defenses, impossible means just that. If the non-breaching party can finish the job, so can the breaching party.

If the question has dollar amounts, state the dollar amounts each party should get (or pay) when discussing remedy.]

Sample Answer 16-6: Common Law Remedies

DOTTIE v. ESTATE OF FESTER

The rights and remedies of the parties here depend on whether there was a valid contract. A CONTRACT is a promise or set of promises the performance of which the law will recognize as a duty and for the breach of which the law will provide a remedy.

1. What are Dottie's remedies at law relative to the stock?

1) UCC?

UCC Article 2 governs contracts for the sale of GOODS. GOODS are movable things at the time of identification to the contract. Otherwise only the common law applies.

Here the contract is not for a sale of goods because it is an exchange of promises that Dottie will provide services and Fester will leave her his stock in his Will in exchange.

Therefore, only the COMMON LAW governs.

2) Is a WRITING REQUIRED?

Under the STATUTE OF FRAUDS certain types of contracts must be in writing to be enforced. A contract for transfer of stock is not one of them.

Therefore, no writing is required by the Statute of Frauds.

3) UNILATERAL CONTRACT?

Under contract law a UNILATERAL CONTRACT is proposed by an offer that unequivocally requires acceptance by performance and cannot be accepted merely by a promise of performance.

Here this offer unequivocally required Dottie to "actually take care of " Fester for the rest of his life because Fester "emphasized" Dottie could not accept by merely "promising" to do what he asked.

Therefore, this was an offer of a unilateral contract.

4) SAVING DOCTRINES of a UNILATERAL CONTRACT?

Under the common law an offeror could revoke her offer at any time before acceptance. Under that view Fester could revoke at any time, leaving Dottie without a remedy. Modernly SAVING DOCTRINES have been adopted to prohibit the offeror of a unilateral contract from revoking for a reasonable time after becoming aware that the offeree has begun performance in acceptance.

Under an alternative view the offeror may revoke but the offeree has a right to RESTITUTION to avoid UNJUST ENRICHMENT.

Here Dottie <u>began performance</u> in acceptance because she "sold her home", "moved" and "nursed Fester." And Fester was <u>aware</u> of her performance because he was alert despite his paralysis.

Therefore, under the modern savings doctrines Dottie would usually be given a reasonable time to complete performance. Here a "reasonable time" is the rest of Fester's life, since that was the condition of the offer.

<u>5) BREACH OF IMPLIED COVENANT?</u>

Under contract law an IMPLIED COVENANT by each party to a contract is that they will not act to prevent the other party from performing contract duties and they will take reasonable steps to assure the other party enjoys the expected benefit of the bargain. Performance of this implied covenant is an IMPLIED MATERIAL CONDITION of every contract,

Here Fester breached the implied covenant because he denied Dottie the opportunity to complete performance in acceptance. This caused a failure of an implied material condition because it <u>totally denied her any of the benefits</u> she expected from the contract.

Therefore, Dottie can claim a MAJOR BREACH by Fester.

<u>6) Dottie's CONTRACT REMEDY?</u>

Under contract law remedies are COMPENSATORY to give the non-breaching party the benefit of the bargain, the compensation that had been bargained for. If property is UNIQUE money damages are in inadequate remedy and SPECIFIC PERFORMANCE is appropriate.

Here the stock is not "unique" and money damages are adequate.

Therefore Dottie's remedy is an award of money damages equal to the value of the stock.

<u>2. What are Dottie's remedies at law relative to the house?</u>

The same common law and savings doctrines apply to the house as for the stock as explained above. But under the STATUTE OF FRAUDS contracts for interests in <u>land</u> must be in writing to be enforced at law.

<u>7) STATUTE OF FRAUDS?</u>

The Statute of Frauds is defined above.

Here the contract was for conveyance of an interest in <u>land</u> because the contract was for a "house" to be given to Dottie in exchange for services.

Therefore, the Statute of Frauds would require a writing, and this contract generally cannot be enforced at law regarding the house.

3. What are Dottie's remedies for enforcement at equity?

8) PROMISSORY ESTOPPEL?

If a plaintiff has no adequate remedy at law, they may be able to obtain a remedy in equity. Here Dottie has an adequate remedy at law as to the promise of the stock, so she cannot seek enforcement at equity as to that part of Fester's promise. But since she has no adequate remedy as to the promise of the house, she can seek a remedy at equity as to that part of her claim.

Under the equitable doctrine of PROMISSORY ESTOPPEL a promise or contract that cannot be enforced at law might be enforced at equity to the extent necessary to prevent unjust enrichment where 1) the party to be bound made a promise ,2) intending to induce reliance, 3) there was reasonable reliance on the promise by the party seeking equity, and 4) justice demands enforcement.

Here there was a promise because Fester "promised" to give Dottie the house. And Fester made the promise intending to induce reliance by Dottie because he wanted her to "move" to where he lived and "nurse" him. Dottie reasonably relied because she trusted him as an "honest, God-fearing Christian." And there would be injustice otherwise because she nursed him for "10 years."

To enforce the promise Dottie would argue that an award of money damages is insufficient to prevent unjust enrichment because the "house" is unique property. A Court of equity may order title to the house conveyed to her (EQUITABLE REPLEVIN) to prevent injustice.

Therefore, Dottie may be able to enforce the promise in equity even though it could not be enforced at law.

4. What are Dottie's remedies in alternative to enforcement?

9) EQUITABLE RESTITUTION?

At equity a party that cannot enforce a promise at law or equity may still seek damages in RESTITUTION to prevent UNJUST ENRICHMENT. The measure of damages may be either the benefits their performance conveyed to the breaching party, or else the detriment they have suffered in reasonable reliance.

Here Dottie can seek RESTITUTION for the benefits she conveyed to Fester. He enjoyed benefits that would have cost him $40,000 a year for ten years, so he enjoyed an unjust enrichment of $400,000.

In the alternative Dottie suffered a loss of $50,000 on her house and foregone wages of $2,500,000 over the ten year period, for a total of $2,550,000.

Dottie may seek an award of money damages in these amounts in equitable restitution.

[**ANSWER EXPLANATION:** This call of this question is for a discussion of REMEDIES and yet the facts raise other issues that should be discussed first such as the Statute of Frauds.

Always follow the call of the question, but you can use "sub-issues" as shown here to discuss necessary issues that the call does not mention.

The first question asked in the call should settle the matter of the stock since Dottie has an adequate legal remedy as to that part of her claim. The last three questions deal with the promise of just the house, and as to that Dottie has no adequate legal remedy because the Statute of Frauds generally bars legal enforcement of an oral contract for conveyance of an interest in land.

Another possible issue here is the “part performance doctrine” under which the Court will legally enforce an oral sales agreement for land in certain very narrow circumstances. The reason I don’t discuss it in my sample answer is that it would so clearly fail that it did not seem an intended issue. That doctrine requires the “buyer” to take possession of the land in a manner that almost unequivocally proves an oral sales agreement. Here Dottie did not take possession; she shared possession. And nothing she did “unequivocally” showed any oral agreement to “sell” the land.

Therefore, it appears Dottie’s only remedies as to the promise of the house are at equity.]

Sample Answer 16-7: UCC Formation, Breach and Remedy

SELLCO v. BUYCO

The rights and remedies of the parties here depend on whether there was a valid contract. A CONTRACT is a promise or set of promises the performance of which the law will recognize as a duty and for the breach of which the law will provide a remedy.

1) Does the UCC apply?

UCC Article 2 governs contracts for the sale of GOODS. GOODS are movable things at the time of identification to the contract.

Here the question involves a sale of "widgets" and they are clearly moveable because they were to be "delivered".

Therefore, Article 2 of UCC applies.

2) Are the parties MERCHANTS?

Under the UCC MERCHANTS are people who deal in the goods or hold themselves out by occupation as knowledgeable about the goods in a contract.

Here Sellco is clearly a dealer in these types of goods because it advertises them in its "catalogue." Buyco is by occupation knowledgeable concerning "widgets" because of the large quantities it is ordering ($60,000).

Therefore, the parties appear to be merchants.

3) Is there a NEED FOR A WRITING?

Under UCC 2-201 a contract for the sale of GOODS over $500 requires a writing signed by the party to be bound unless an exception applies. This limit is being raised to $5,000 but many States are continuing to use the $500 limit.

In a contract between MERCHANTS the need for a writing may be satisfied by a sales confirmation indicating the quantity sent to one party by the other if the receiving party has reason to know the contents of the writing and does not object to the representation of a contract within 10 days.

Here a writing is needed because the cost of the goods is $60,000 ("10,000" at "$6"). But this is "between merchants" because both parties appear to be merchants, and the 6/4 sales confirmation Sellco sent to Buyco specifies quantity at "10,000". That satisfies the requirement of 2-201.

Therefore a writing was needed, but the need for a writing would be satisfied by the 6/4 message, unless Buyco objected within 10 days.

4) Was the catalogue an OFFER?

Under contract law an OFFER is a manifestation of present contractual intent communicated to the offeree that is so specific that an objective observer would reasonably believe assent would form a bargain. An advertisement is never a valid offer unless it clearly identifies the QUANTITY of goods for sale and the PARTY to whom the offeror is willing to sell them.

Here the catalogue is not an offer because it is just a price list that does not specify the quantity of any product Sellco is willing to sell. No reasonable person would believe merely 'assenting' to the catalogue would alone form a bargain, so a catalogue cannot be an 'offer'..

Therefore, the catalogue itself is not an offer.

5) 6/2/99 OFFER by Buyco?

Offer is defined above.

Here the communication from Buyco expresses present contractual intent because it says "we hereby accept". The offer is specific as to parties because it says "we" and "your", and it is specific as to a quantity of "10,000". This is specific enough for an offer because it objectively appears assent would form a bargain.

Therefore, this is a valid offer.

6) 6/3/99 ACCEPTANCE?

Under UCC 2-206 an offer that does not clearly require acceptance in a specific manner can be accepted in any reasonable manner including a promise to ship or shipment of conforming or non-conforming goods.

Under UCC 2-207 an acceptance that includes varying terms is still effective. If the contract is between merchants the varying term proposed by the offeree may become part of the contract if the offer did not expressly require acceptance according to its terms, the offeror does not object to the varying terms within a reasonable time, and the varying terms are not a material alteration of the offer terms.

Even when varying terms do not automatically become part of the contract they may become part of the contract by agreement, and the UCC allows modification without additional consideration.

Here Sellco did not promise to ship in response to Buyco's offer because it said it "could provide" and not that it "would" provide the product. The word "could" does not imply any "promise to ship". Therefore the response of Sellco was a rejection of Buyco's offer and and a counter-offer to sell on different terms.

Buyco's reaction to Sellco's offer to sell without warranty was an acceptance because Buyco "verbally agreed."

Even if one argues that Sellco accepted Buyco's offer with a varying term, Buyco still "agreed" to it, so that would have modified the contract to exclude the warranty term anyway.

Therefore, there was an acceptance under either interpretation, and there is "no warranty" under either interpretation.

7) <u>TERMS?</u>

Under UCC Article 2 a goods contract is enforceable if <u>quantity and parties are specified</u>.. All other terms can be supplied by the UCC's GAP FILLERS.

Here the <u>parties</u> are specified as Sellco and Buyco. The <u>quantity</u> is 10,000 yellow widgets at a price of $6 without a warranty for delivery on 6/8.

Therefore the contract is specific enough to be enforced.

8) <u>BREACH?</u>

Under the PERFECT TENDER RULE of the UCC goods must be supplied <u>exactly as ordered</u>. Any non-conforming delivery is a major breach.

A seller that delivers non-conforming goods has a right to GIVE NOTICE of intent to cure, and may CURE the shipment of non-conforming goods at any time within the contract period. Further, the seller gets a reasonable amount of extra time beyond the contract period if the original shipment was sent with a <u>reasonable belief it would satisfy the buyer's needs</u>.

Here Sellco <u>shipped non-conforming goods</u> because it shipped "blue widgets". They were not sent with a reasonable belief they would satisfy the buyer's needs because they were sent by " mistake". And there is no time left to cure in the contract period because the shipment was on the deadline of "6/8/99", and

Therefore, Sellco breached by shipping non-conforming goods, and has no time left to cure.

9) <u>Buyco's REMEDY?</u>

Under the UCC a buyer who receives nonconforming goods can REJECT the goods and REPUDIATE the contract. The buyer can COVER by buying the goods elsewhere and demand the excess of the cover price over the contract price, or demand the excess of market price over the contract price.

Here Buyco had a right to reject the goods, and it covered at a price of $5. Since this is less than the $6 contract price, Buyco has suffered <u>no loss</u> as a result of the breach and has no right to receive damages from Sellco.

Therefore, Buyco's demand for $50,000 has no basis and they would get nothing.

[**ANSWER EXPLANATION:** This is a simple UCC formation, breach and remedy question. The need for writing, and the existence of a writing must be discussed.

If an offeree says it "will" or "would" ship goods it is a promise to ship and an acceptance, even if they cite a varying term. In this case UCC 2-207 applies. But if the offeree only says it "can" or "could" ship on different terms it is not a promise to ship. It is really a rejection and counter-offer.

The unusual fact here is that Buyco has suffered no loss, so they can recover no damages. This should be expressly recognized. They promised to buy for $6 and they covered for $5. They benefited from Sellco's error and have no cause of action.]

Index

N

O

P

Q

R

S

T

U

W

Y